Table of Contents

ESSENTIAL EARLY CHILDHOOD SKILLS

The activities in *Everything for Early Learning* are designed to help your child develop the following reading, language and mathematics skills:

READING

The activities in this section are designed to help your child:

- recognize the letter/sound association of consonants and vowels
- discriminate likenesses and differences in those sounds
- use letters and sounds to read words, sentences and stories
- understand and identify the key components of a sentence
- write his/her own sentences and brief stories
- identify and use punctuation correctly
- develop a variety of specific reading comprehension skills

LANGUAGE

The activities in this section are designed to help your child:

- understand and use the basic parts of speech (nouns, verbs, adjectives)
- develop basic alphabetization and dictionary skills
- develop skill in classifying pictures, words and ideas

ESSENTIAL EARLY CHILDHOOD SKILLS

Math

The activities in this section are designed to help your child:

- develop appropriate mathematical language
- use cardinal and ordinal numbers
- add and subtract numbers ranging from one to three digits
- identify the place value of numbers through the thousands place
- practice multiplication facts through 10 x 10
- identify and use basic geometrical shapes
- identify and write simple fractions
- practice measurement skills with inches and centimeters
- tell time to the hour, half-hour and quarter-hour
- identify and count pennies, nickels, dimes and quarters

CONSONANTS

Beginning Consonant

You can keep **b**uns in a **b**asket.

basket

Look at the pictures that show how baskets can be used. Say each picture name. If the picture name **begins** with the same sound as **buns** and **basket**, **color** it.

Beginning Consonant

Carla is looking for a team **c**ap.

cap

Cut out the pictures at the bottom. Say each picture name. If the picture **begins** with the same sound as **cap**, **glue** it on a cap.

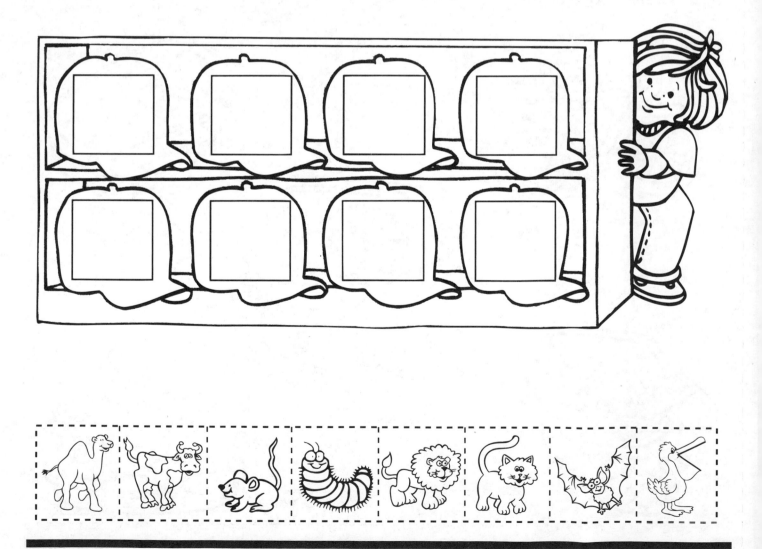

Beginning Consonant

Doughnut ice cream is my favorite **d**essert!

doughnuts

Cut out the pictures at the bottom. Say each picture name. If the picture name **begins** with the same sound as **doughnuts**, **glue** it on the dish of doughnut ice cream.

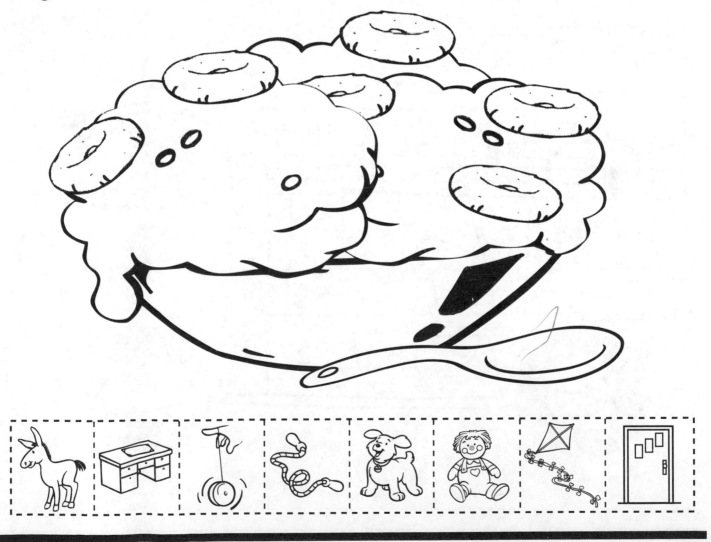

Beginning Consonant Ff

Find the number on the **f**irefighter's truck.

firefighter

Say each picture name. If the picture name **begins** with the same sound as **firefighter**, **color** the space. What did you find?

Beginning Consonant

What **g**ift did the **g**irl **g**et?

gift

Say each picture name. **Color** the space if the picture name **begins** with the same sound as **gift**. What gift did the girl get?

Beginning Consonant Hh

Who is **h**iding in the farmer's **h**ay?

hay

Say each picture name. **Color** the space if the picture name **begins** with the same sound as **hay**. What animal is hiding in the hay?

Beginning Consonant Jj

Jack put too much **j**unk in his **j**eep.

jeep

Say the picture name for each piece of junk in Jack's jeep. If the picture name **begins** with the same sound as **jeep**, **write** a **j** on it.

Beginning Consonant Kk
Look at the **k**ites in the big tree!

kite

Cut out the pictures at the bottom. Say each picture name. If the picture name **begins** with the same sound as **kite**, **glue** it on a kite in the tree.

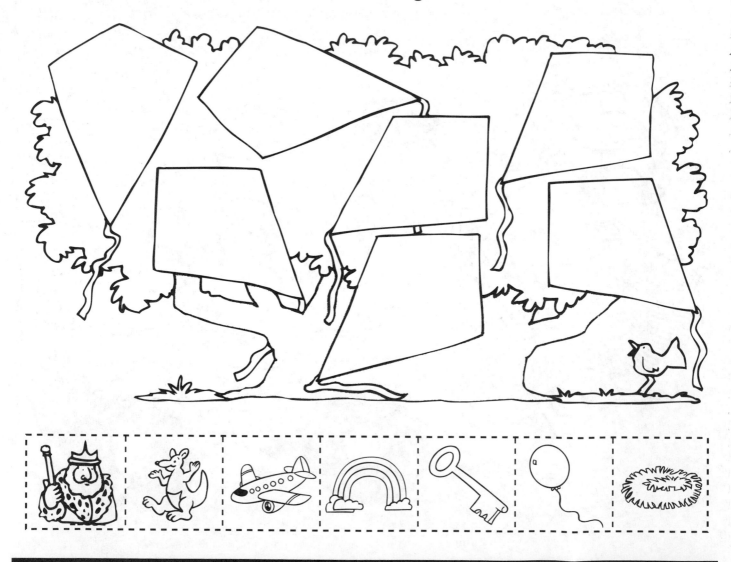

Beginning Consonant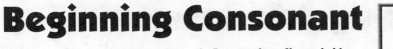

Help the **l**ittle **l**ost **l**amb find its mother.

lamb

Cut out the picture of the lamb at the bottom. Use the picture to follow the path to its mother. Each time you pass a picture whose name **begins** with the same sound as **lamb**, **write** an **l** on it. When you are through, **glue** the baby next to its mother.

Beginning Consonant Mm

How **m**any **m**onkeys **m**eet at the **m**ovie?

 **m**onkeys

Cut out the pictures at the bottom. **Glue** them beside things in the picture whose names **begin** with the same sound as **monkeys**.

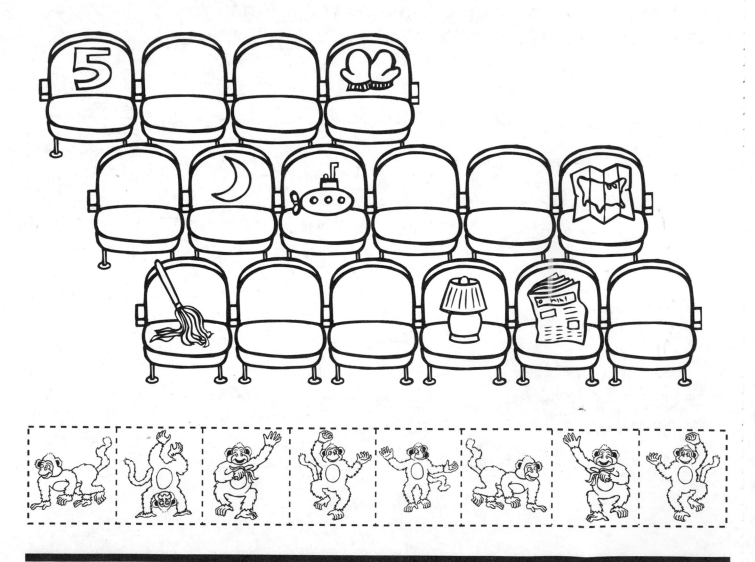

Beginning Consonant Nn

Can you make a **n**ecklace out of **n**uts?

necklace

Say the picture name on each nut on the necklace. If the picture sound **begins** with the same sound as **necklace, color** the nut.

Beginning Consonant P p
Come to **P**ete's **p**izza **p**arty!

pizza

Pete is so picky he only serves foods whose names begin with the same sound as **pizza** at his party. What else does Pete serve? Say the picture names. **Draw** a line from Pete to each picture whose name **begins** with the same sound as **pizza**.

Beginning Consonant

How **qu**ickly can you decorate the **qu**een's crown?

queen

Cut out the pictures at the bottom. Say each picture name. If the picture name **begins** with the same sound as **queen**, **glue** it on her crown.

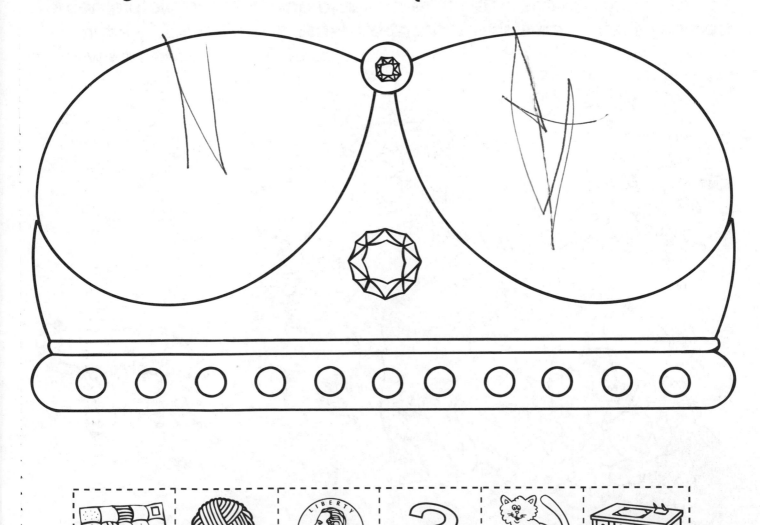

Beginning Consonant

Welcome to the **r**emarkable
animal **r**anch. Look! There's a
rabbit **r**acing on **r**oller skates!

rabbit

Say the picture name of each remarkable animal. If the picture name
begins with the same sound as **rabbit**, **write** an **r** on it.

Beginning Consonant

On **s**unny days, **S**umi plays in her **s**andbox.

sandbox

Sumi only plays with things that begin with the same sound as **sandbox**. Say the picture names. **Draw** a line from Sumi to each picture whose name **begins** with the same sound as **sandbox**.

Beginning Consonant **Tt**

Tune in **t**o your favorite **t**elevision show.

television

Cut out the pictures at the bottom. Say each picture name. If the picture name **begins** with the same sound as **television**, **glue** it on the television.

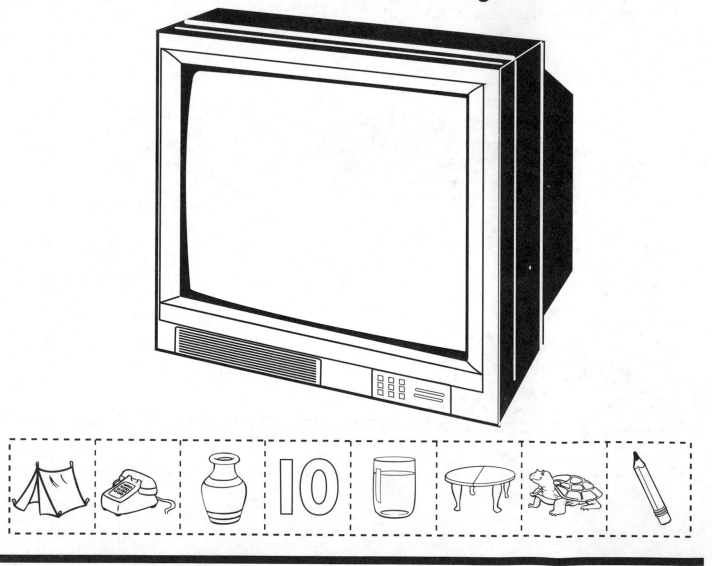

Beginning Consonant

Look out! The **v**olcano is ready to erupt!

volcano

Cut out the pictures at the bottom. Say each picture name. If the picture name **begins** with the same sound as **volcano**, **glue** it on the volcano.

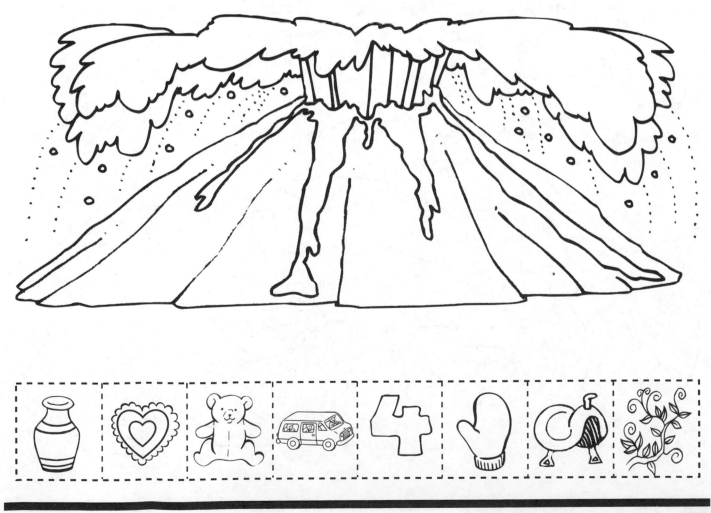

Beginning Consonant Ww

Winnie **W**alrus **w**ants you to play in the **w**aves.

walrus

Help Winnie get to the ocean water. **Draw** a line to follow the path with the pictures whose names **begin** with the same sound as **walrus**.

Consonant Xx

Re**x** is si**x** today.

6 six

The word **six** ends with the sound that the letter **x** stands for. Help Rex get to his birthday cake. **Draw** a line to follow the path with the pictures whose names **end** with the same sounds as **six**.

Beginning Consonant

Yvette knits a **y**arn blanket for her great-grandmother.

yarn

Say the picture names in each square on Yvette's blanket. **Circle** the picture whose name **begins** with the same sound as **yarn**.

Beginning Consonant Zz

Step inside the **z**any **z**oo!

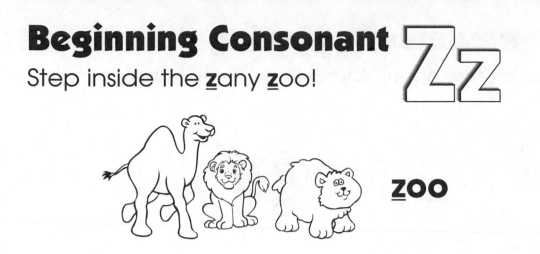

ZOO

Circle the zany pictures whose names **begin** with the same sound as **zoo**.

Review: Beginning Consonants

Say each picture name. **Circle** the letter that stands for the **beginning sound**.

p m n

v t s

f g p

s c p

m g v

g p n

m p n

t g p

s l c

g f c

p b f

v l t

Review: Beginning Consonants

Look at the letters in the boxes. Then, say each picture name. **Draw** a line from the letter to the picture whose name **begins** with that sound.

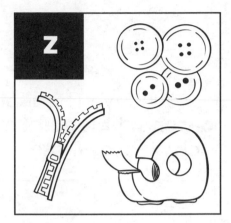

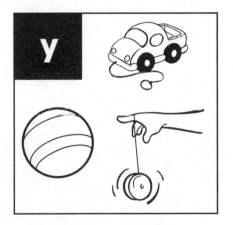

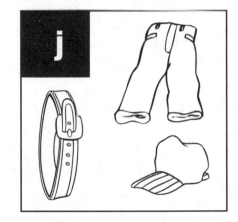

Beginning Consonant Blends

Consonant blends are two consonants that join to form a single sound.

The **fr**og **st**opped on the **pl**ant.

The sounds you hear at the beginning of **frog, stopped** and **plant** are **consonant blends**. Say the name of the first picture in each row. **Circle** each picture whose name **begins** with the same blend.

fruit

star

plant

clock

Beginning Consonant Blends:
bl, cl, fl, gl, pl, sl

Draw a circle around the **beginning blend** for each picture.

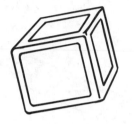

bl fl cl

cl fl gl

fl bl pl

fl cl gl

pl gl cl

sl fl gl

gl fl cl

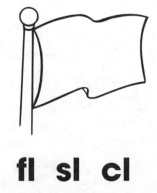

fl sl cl

cl gl sl

Beginning Consonant Blends:
bl, sl, cr, cl

Look at the pictures and say their names. **Write** the beginning consonant blend for each picture.

 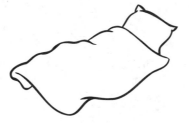 

___ **own**   ___ **anket**   ___ **ayon**

___ **ock**   ___ **ide**   ___ **oud**

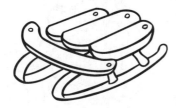  

___ **ed**   ___ **ab**   ___ **ocodile**

Beginning Consonant Blends:
br, fr, gr, pr, tr

Look at the pictures and say their names. **Write** the beginning consonant blend for each picture.

_____   _____   _____

_____   _____   _____

_____   _____   _____

Consonants

Beginning Consonant Blends:
br, cr, dr, fr, pr

The beginning blend for each word is missing. **Write** in the correct blend to finish the word. **Draw** a line from the word to its picture.

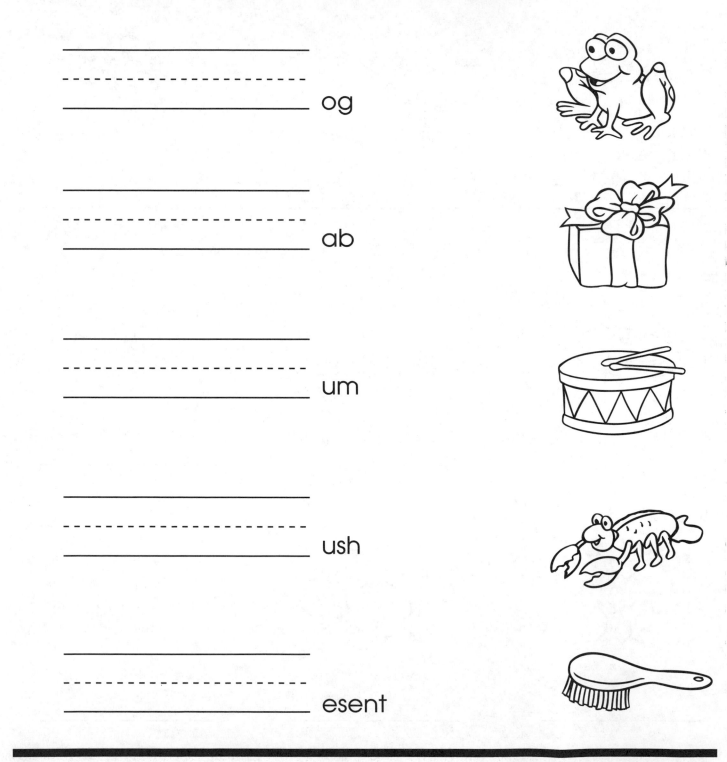

_____
- - - - - - - - - - - - - -
_____ og

_____
- - - - - - - - - - - - - -
_____ ab

_____
- - - - - - - - - - - - - -
_____ um

_____
- - - - - - - - - - - - - -
_____ ush

_____
- - - - - - - - - - - - - -
_____ esent

Beginning Consonant Blends

Read the words. Listen for the blend at the beginning of each word.

tree   **bread**   **crown**   **frog**   **grapes**   **price**

Look at the letters on the presents. Find the pictures below that **begin** with the sounds that the letters stand for. **Glue** them where they belong.

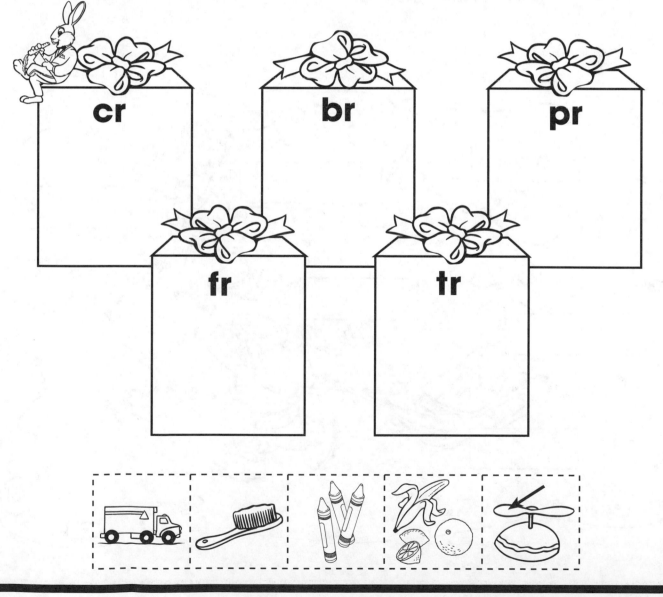

Beginning Consonant Blends

Read the words in the box. Then, look at the picture. Use the words in the box to **label** the picture. The first one shows you what to do.

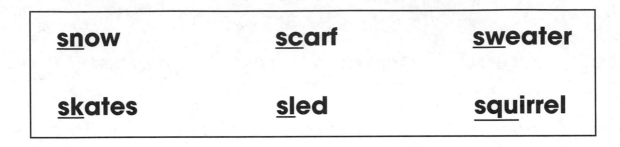

snow	**s**carf	**s**weater
skates	**sl**ed	**s**quirrel

Beginning Consonant Blends:
fl, br, pl, sk, sn

Look at the pictures and say their names. **Write** the beginning consonant blend for each picture.

Beginning Consonant Blends

Cut out the train and the smoke stack. Cut on the dotted lines to make slits on the train. Slide the smoke stack and read each word.

Example:

ain

| br | dr | gr | pl | str | tr |

Review: Beginning Consonant Blends

Read each sentence. **Circle** the word that completes each sentence.
Write the word on the line.

dream
stream
clean

_____

- - - - - - - - - - - - - - - - -

1. I like to sit and _____ about what I want to be.

sleep
spell
street

_____

- - - - - - - - - - - - - - - - -

2. I could teach children to read and _____ .

store
step
flame

_____

- - - - - - - - - - - - - - - - -

3. It would be fun to own a _____ .

plant
dress
star

_____

- - - - - - - - - - - - - - - - -

4. Maybe I will be a big movie _____ .

smile
grill
small

_____

- - - - - - - - - - - - - - - - -

5. That dream really makes me _____ !

Ending Consonant Blends: ft, lt

Write lt or **ft** to complete the words.

be _____

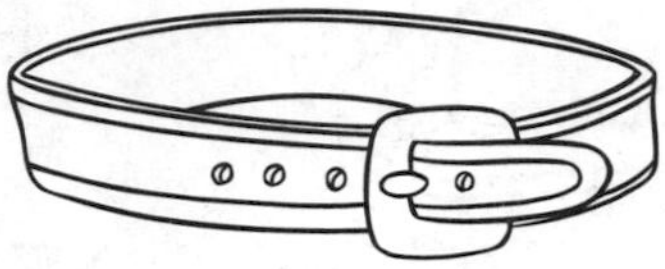

ra _____

sa _____

qui _____

gi _____

Ending Consonant Blends:
lf, lk, sk, sp, st

Draw a line from the picture to the blend that **ends** the word.

lf

lk

sk

sp

st

Ending Consonant Blends:
mp, nd, nk, ng

In every box, there is a word ending and a list of letters. **Add** each of the letters to the word ending to make rhyming words.

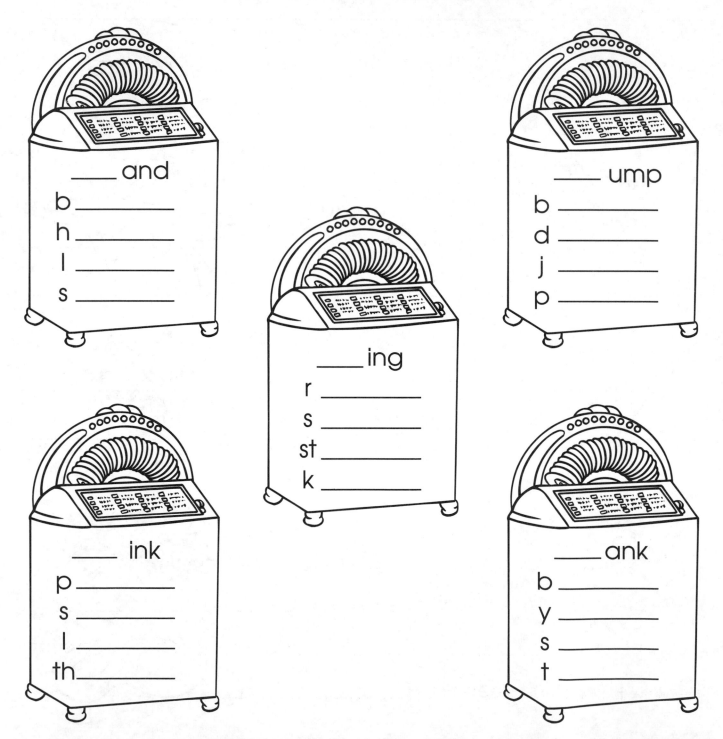

_____ and

b _____
h _____
l _____
s _____

_____ ump

b _____
d _____
j _____
p _____

_____ ing

r _____
s _____
st _____
k _____

_____ ink

p _____
s _____
l _____
th _____

_____ ank

b _____
y _____
s _____
t _____

Ending Consonant Blends: ng and nk

Look at the words in the word box. **Write** all of the words that **end** with the **ng** sound under the picture of the **ring**. **Write** all of the words that **end** with the **nk** sound under the picture of the **sink**. Finish the sentences with words from the word box.

strong	king	bring	bank	honk
long	sank	thank	stung	bunk

ng

nk

_____   _____

_____   _____

_____   _____

_____   _____

_____   _____

1. _____ your horn when you get to my house.

2. He was _____ by a bumblebee.

3. We are going to put our money in a _____ .

4. I want to _____ you for the birthday present.

5. My brother and I sleep in _____ beds.

Beginning Consonant Digraphs

Let's visit the **ch**icks and **sh**eep at the petting farm.

chicks   **sheep**

The letters at the beginning of the words **chicks** and **sheep** are called **consonant digraphs**. The two consonants join together to form one new sound.

Cut out the pictures at the bottom. Say each picture name. If the picture name **begins** with the same sound as **chicks**, **glue** it near the chicks. If the picture name **begins** with the same sound as **sheep**, **glue** it near the sheep.

Beginning Consonant Digraphs

Thirteen swimmers saw the huge **wh**ale.

Thirteen

whale

Say each picture name. If you hear the sound at the beginning of the word **thirteen, write th** on the line. **Write wh** if you hear the sound at the beginning of the word **whale**.

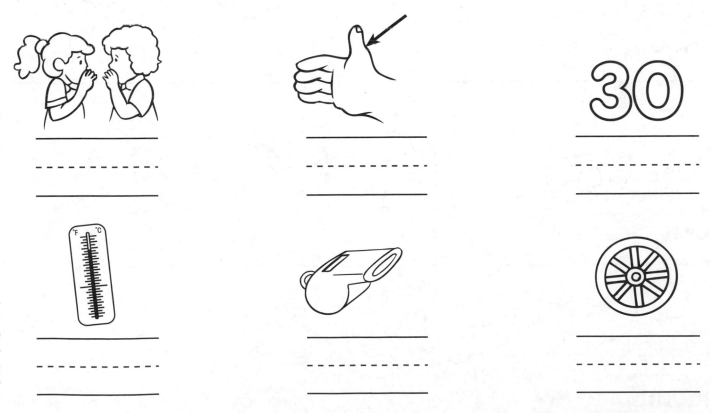

Beginning Consonant Digraphs:
wh, sh, ch, th

Look at the first picture in each row and say its name. **Circle** the pictures that have the same sound.

whistle

shoe

chin

thumb

Beginning Consonant Digraphs:
wh, sh, ch, th

Look at the pictures and say their names. **Write** the beginning consonant digraph for each picture.

_____

_____

_____

_____

_____

_____

_____

_____

_____

Ending Consonant Digraphs:
sh, ch, ck

Jo**sh** looks at the clo**ck**.

Say each picture name. **Write** the consonant digraph you hear at the **end** of each picture name.

TRUCK

Review: Consonant Digraphs

Read the words in the box. Then, look at the picture. Use the words in the box to **label** the picture. The first one shows you what to do.

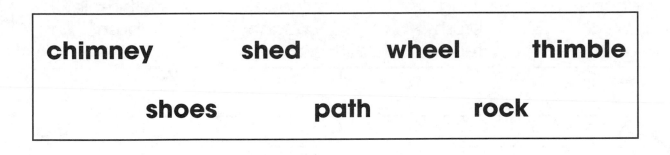

chimney	**shed**	**wheel**	**thimble**
shoes	**path**	**rock**	

shed

Review: Consonant Digraphs

Write the word from the word box next to its picture. **Underline** the consonant digraph in each word.

bench	wing	shoe	thimble
shell	brush	peach	bush
whale	teeth	chair	wheel

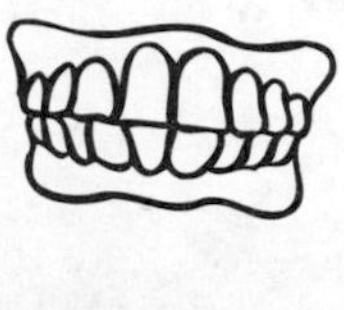

AEIOU

VOWELS

Short Vowel a

How many people can fit in a van?

van

Short a is the sound you hear in the middle of the word **van**. Use a toy car or pretend your finger is a van at the top of the hill. Smoothly move your finger down the hill as you blend the letter sounds to read each word. Then, **write** the word on the line.

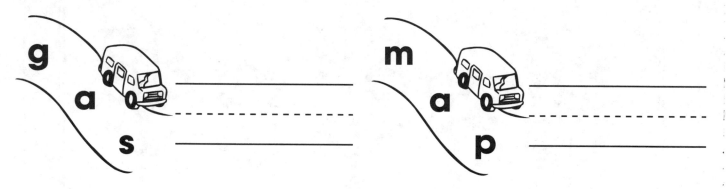

g
a
s

m
a
p

Write the word from above that names each picture.

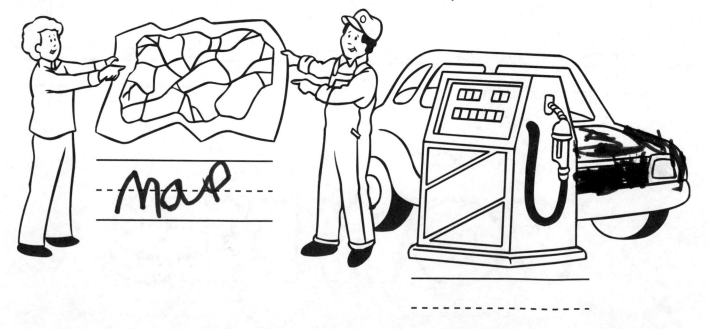

map

Short Vowel a

Say each picture name. **Write a** if you hear the **short a** sound.

m ___ p   h ___ m   c ___ p

b ___ b   f ___ x   c ___ t

Blend the letter sounds to read each word. Then, **trace** the word on the line.

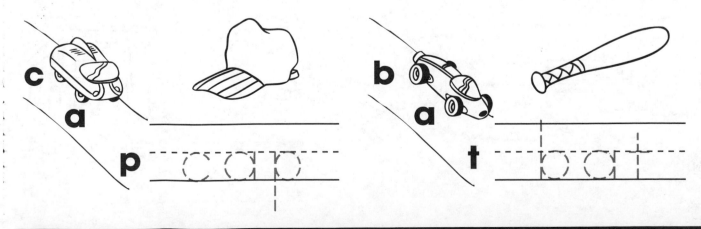

c
a
p   cap

b
a
t   bat

Short Vowel e
Help the r**e**d h**e**n find her **e**ggs.

h**e**n

Short e is the sound you hear in the middle of the word **hen**. **Draw** a line to follow the path with the pictures whose names have the **short e** sound.

Short Vowel e

Blend the letter sounds to read each word. **Write** the word on the line. Then, **write** the word that names each picture at the bottom.

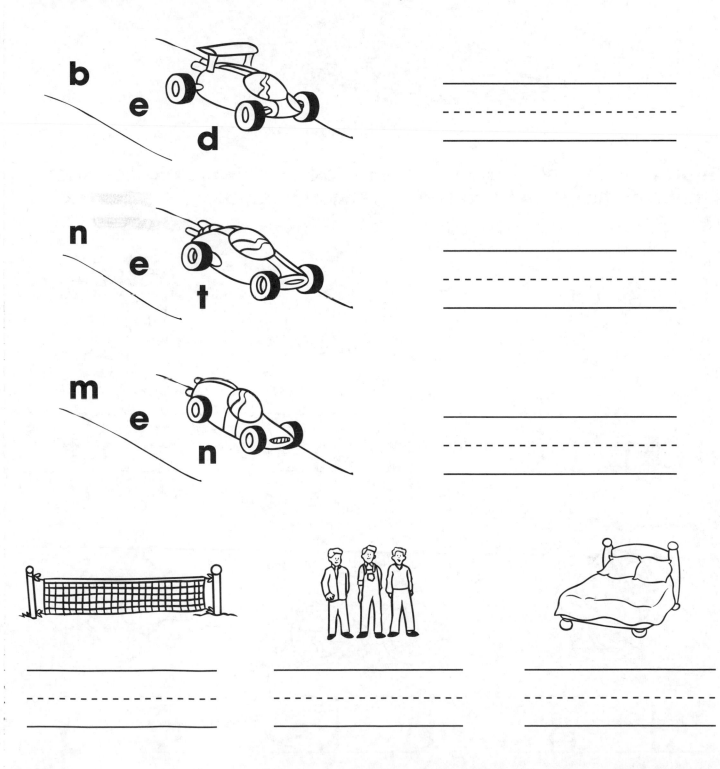

Short Vowel i
This p<u>i</u>g likes to d<u>i</u>g and d<u>i</u>g.

pig

Short i is the sound you hear in the middle of the word **pig**. Say each picture name. **Write i** if you hear the **short i** sound.

ch __ ck

p __ n

g __ ft

f __ n

b __ ke

w __ g

Short Vowel i

Blend the letter sounds to read each word. **Write** the word on the line.

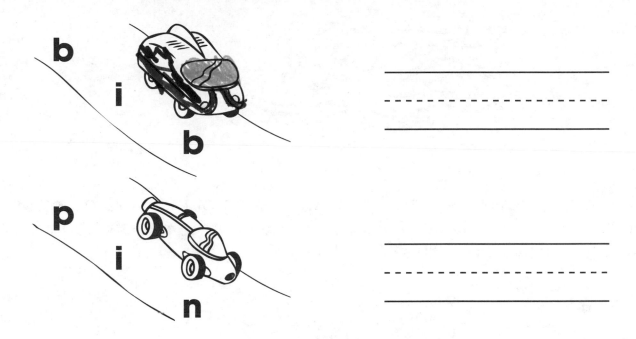

b
i
b

_____

- - - - - - - - - - - - - - - - - -

_____

p
i
n

_____

- - - - - - - - - - - - - - - - - -

_____

Write the word from above that names each picture. Then, find three other things in the picture whose names have the **short i** sound and **circle** them.

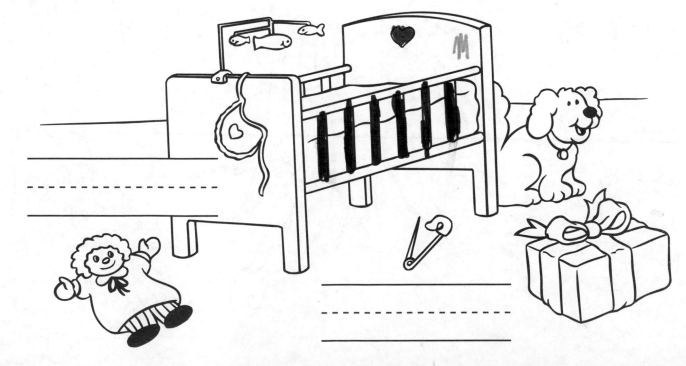

_____

- - - - - - - - - - - - - - - - - -

_____

_____

- - - - - - - - - - - - - - - - - -

_____

Short Vowel o
The **o**ctopus wants s**o**cks.

octopus

Short o is the sound you hear at the beginning of the word **octopus**. Say each picture name. **Color** the sock if you hear the **short o** sound. Does this octopus have enough colored socks?

Short Vowel o

Say each picture name. **Write o** if you hear the **short o** sound.

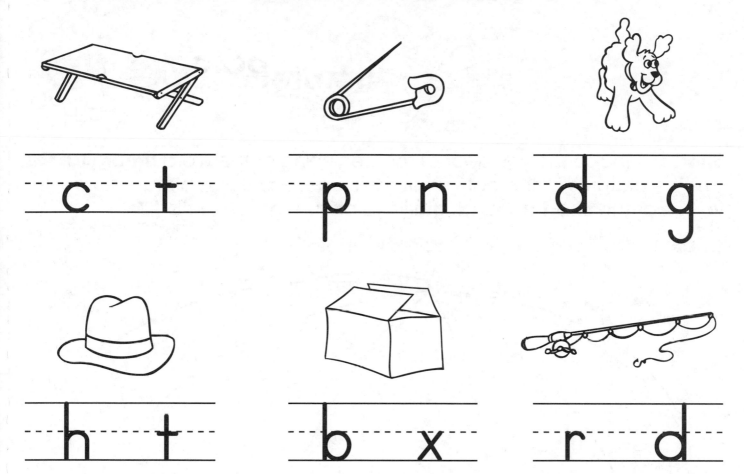

c _ t   p _ n   d _ g

h _ t   b _ x   r _ d

Blend the letter sounds to read each word. Then, **trace** the word on the line.

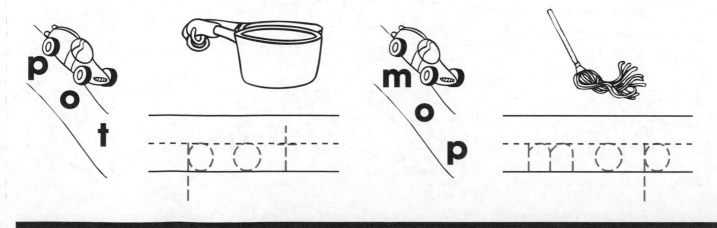

p o t   _____   m o p

Short Vowel u
Decorate the big beach **u**mbrella.

umbrella

Short u is the sound you hear at the beginning of the word **umbrella**. **Cut out** the pictures at the bottom of the page. Say each picture name. If you hear the **short u** sound, **glue** the picture on the umbrella.

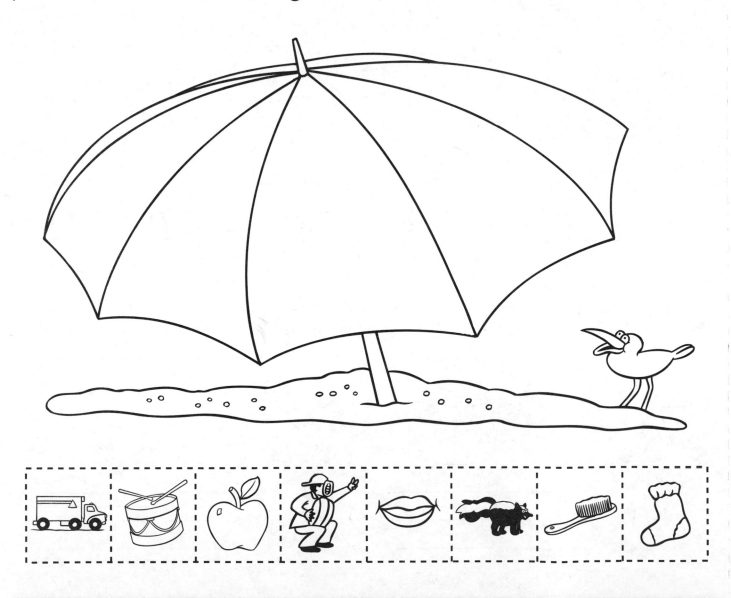

Short Vowel u

Blend the letter sounds to read each word. **Write** the word on the line.

_____

- - - - - - - - - - - - - -

_____

_____

- - - - - - - - - - - - - -

_____

_____

- - - - - - - - - - - - - -

_____

Write the word from above that names each picture.

_____

- - - - - - - - - - - - - -

_____

_____

- - - - - - - - - - - - - -

_____

Short Vowel Sounds

Say the name of each picture. The short vowel sound may be at the beginning or in the middle of the word. **Color** the pictures in each row that have the same short vowel sound.

Short Vowel Sounds

The words that name the pictures have missing letters. **Write a**, **e**, **i**, **o** or **u** to finish the words.

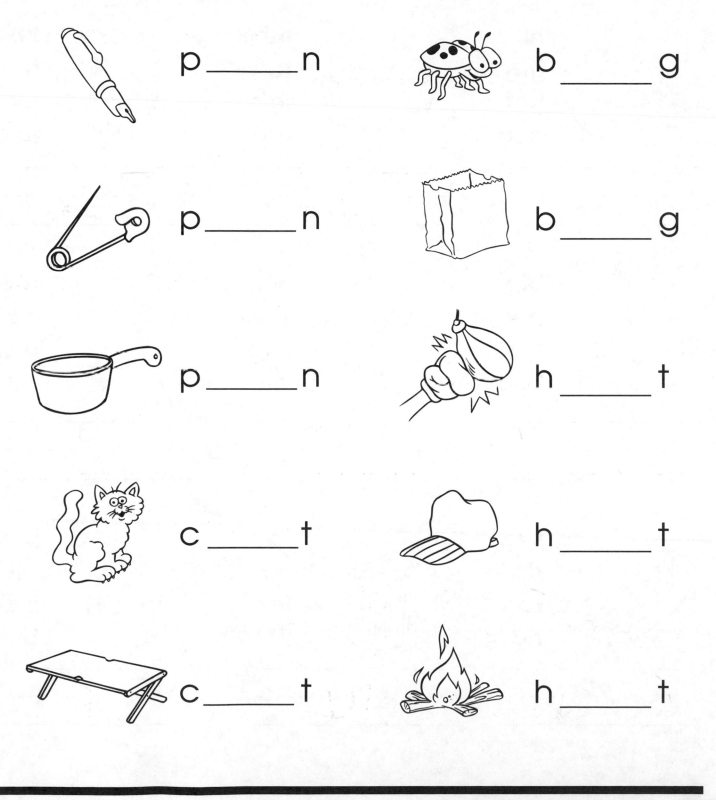

p____n   b____g

p____n   b____g

p____n   h____t

c____t   h____t

c____t   h____t

Short Vowels

Say the name of each picture. **Circle** the picture name. **Write** the name.
The first one shows you what to do.

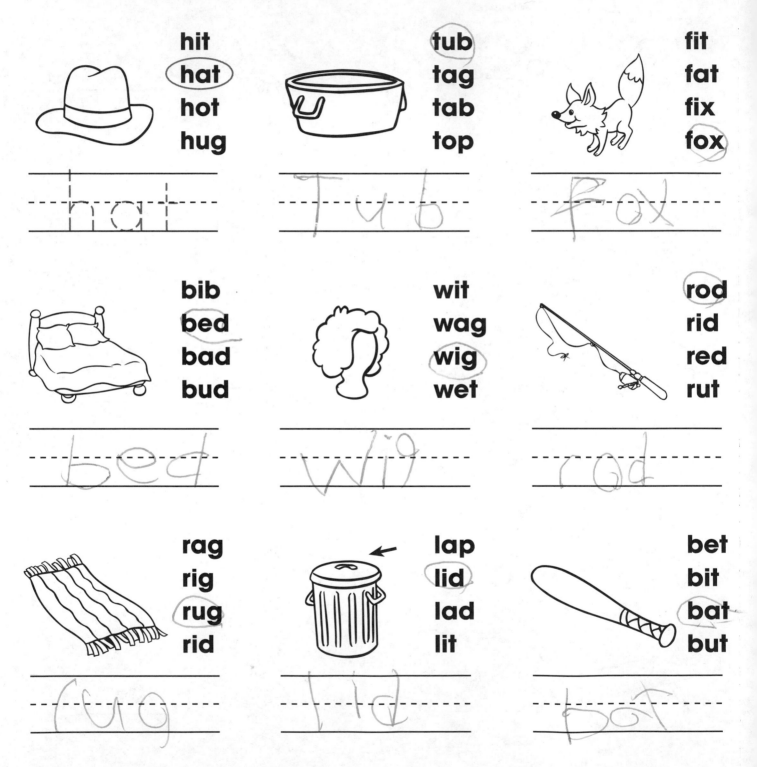

hit
(hat)
hot
hug

hat

tub
tag
tab
top

Tub

fit
fat
fix
(fox)

Fox

bib
bed
bad
bud

bed

wit
wag
(wig)
wet

wig

(rod)
rid
red
rut

rod

rag
rig
(rug)
rid

rug

lap
(lid)
lad
lit

lid

bet
bit
(bat)
but

bat

Sound Pattern -at

P<u>at</u> wears her favorite **h<u>at</u>** to the costume party.

hat

Cut out the hat and feather. **Cut on** the dotted lines to make slits. **Slip** the feather through the hat. **Slide** the feather up and down to read each word.

Example:

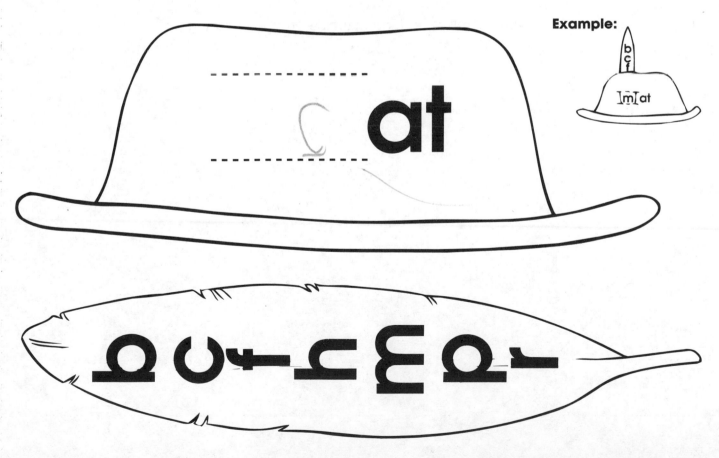

Page is blank for cutting exercise on previous page.

Sound Pattern -in

Put used paper in the recycling b**in**.

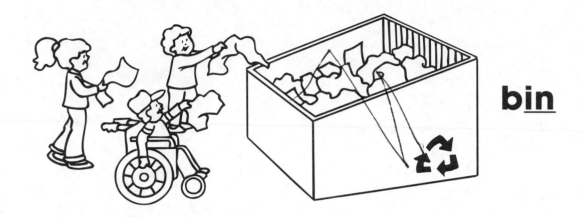

bin

Cut out the bin and paper. **Cut on** the dotted lines to make slits. **Slip** the paper through the slits on the bin. **Slide** the paper up and down to read each word.

Example:

Page is blank for cutting exercise on previous page.

Sound Pattern -ot

The t**ot** naps on a c**ot**.

You can make a flip book to help you read words. **Cut out** the cards. Put the big card with the word **cot** on the bottom. Put the letter cards on top of the big card. **Staple** the cards on the far left side. Then, **flip** the cards and read each word.

Your finished flip book will look like this:

Page is blank for cutting exercise on previous page.

Review: Sound Patterns

The t**ot** and the c**at** reach for the t**in**.

Name each picture. **Cut out** the words at the bottom. **Glue** each word where it belongs.

| hat | tot | cot | fin | mat |

Page is blank for cutting exercise on previous page.

Sound Pattern -it

K**it** will s**it** and read a little flip book.

sit

You can make a flip book to help you read words. **Cut out** the cards. Put the big card with the word **sit** on the bottom. Put the letter cards on top of the big card. **Staple** the cards on the far left side. Then, **flip** the cards and read each word.

Your finished flip book will look like this:

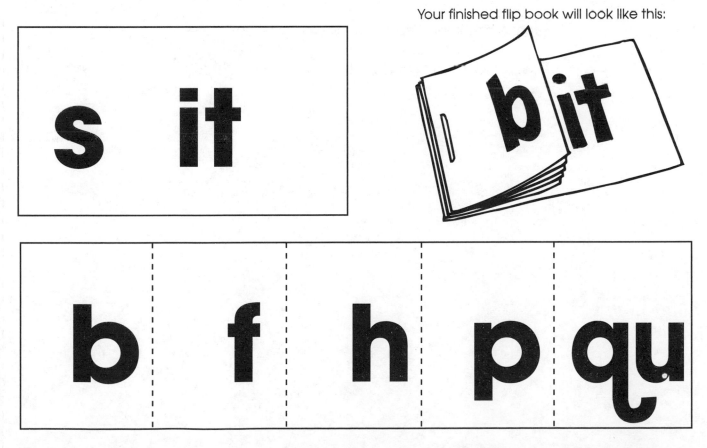

Page is blank for cutting exercise on previous page.

Sound Pattern -ub

The s<u>ub</u> is going under!

sub

Cut out the sub and the scope. **Cut on** the dotted lines to make slits. **Slip** the scope through the slits on the sub. **Slide** the scope up and down to read each word.

Example:

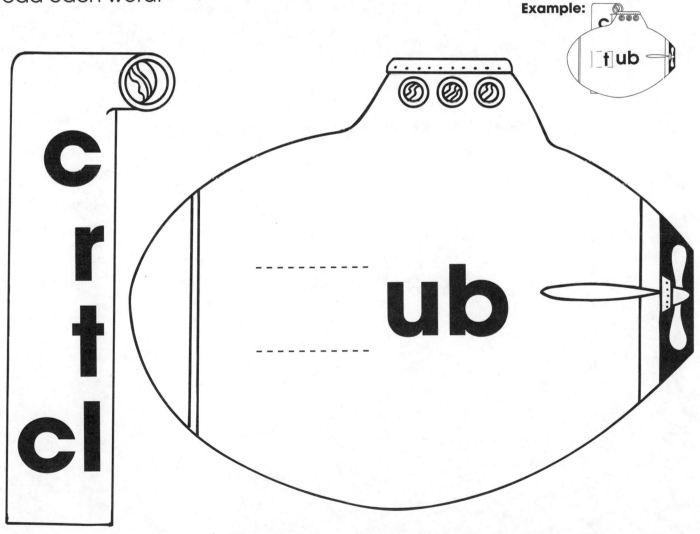

Page is blank for cutting exercise on previous page.

Sound Pattern -ug

Can you find the b**ug** in this r**ug**?

bug

Cut out the wheels. Put the little wheel on top of the big wheel. **Push** a toothpick or a ballpoint pen through the center. Turn the little wheel to read each word.

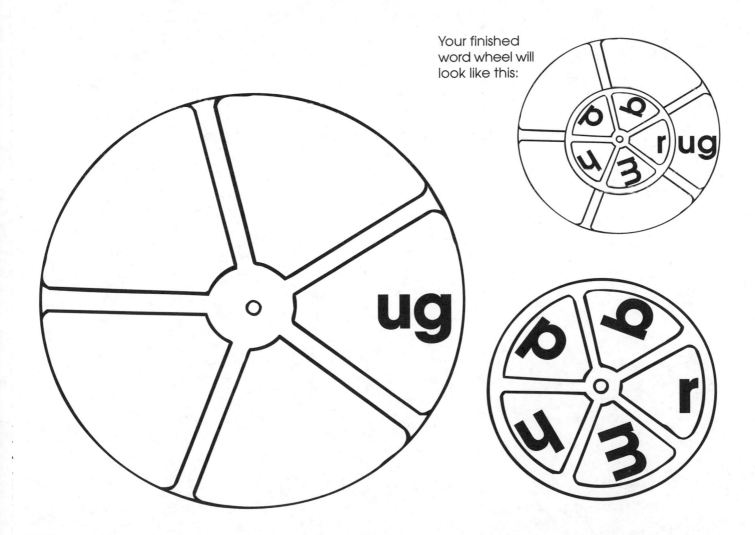

Your finished word wheel will look like this:

Page is blank for cutting exercise on previous page.

Sound Pattern -en

K**en** has t**en** crayons.

ten

You can make a flip book to help you read words. **Cut out** the cards. Put the big card with the word **ten** on the bottom. Put the letter cards on top of the big card. **Staple** the cards on the far left side. Then, **flip** the cards and read each word.

Your finished flip book will look like this:

Page is blank for cutting exercise on previous page.

Review: Sound Patterns

Say the picture names. Read each question. **Circle** the word that answers the question. Then, **write** the word.

Is it a **mug** or a **rug**? _____

Is it **ten** or a **tan**? _____

Is it a **bug** or a **tug**? _____

Is it a **hen** or a **hug**? _____

Is it a **pen** or a **cot**? _____

Review: Sound Patterns

Read each sentence. **Circle** and **write** the word that completes each sentence.

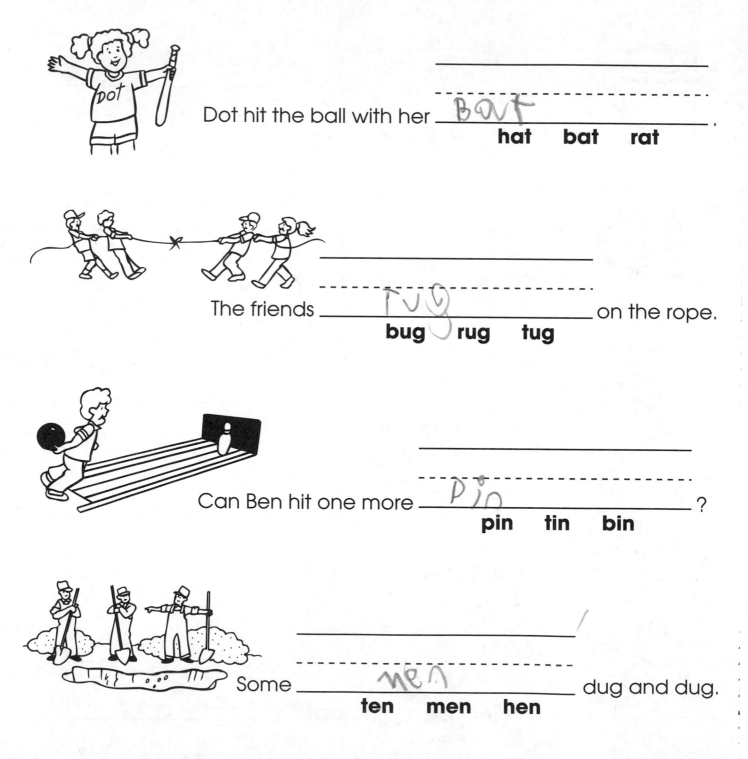

Dot hit the ball with her _Bat_ .

hat   bat   rat

The friends _rug_ on the rope.

bug   rug   tug

Can Ben hit one more _Pin_ ?

pin   tin   bin

Some _hen_ dug and dug.

ten   men   hen

Long Vowel a

Can you pl**ay** the tr**ai**n g**a**m**e** on this tr**ay**?

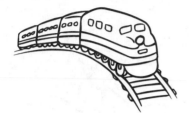

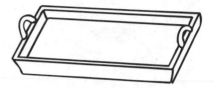

trai**n**   **g**a**m**e**   **tr**ay****

Long a is the sound you hear in the words **train, game** and **tray**. Say each picture name on the game. **Circle** the picture if you hear the **long a** sound.

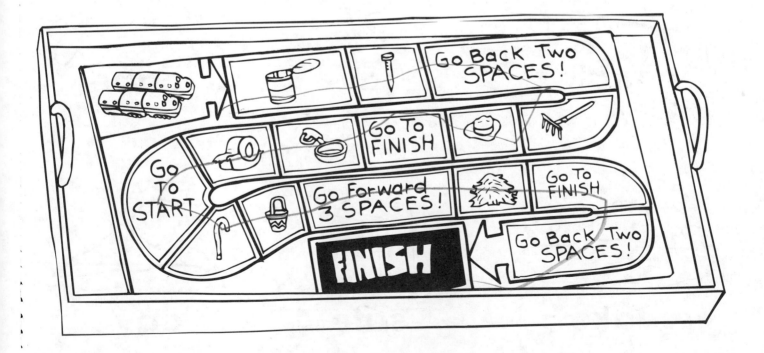

Long Vowel a

Say the name of each picture. **Circle** the letters that make the **long a** sound in the picture name. The first ones show you what to do.

v a s e   s a i l   p a y

mail   jay   cape

lake   safe   day

Long Vowel a

Help J**ay** s**ai**l across the l**a**k**e** to the c**a**v**e**.

Read the words on Jay's sail. Then, look at the pictures on the maze. Use the words on the sail to **label** the pictures on the maze. The first one shows you what to do.

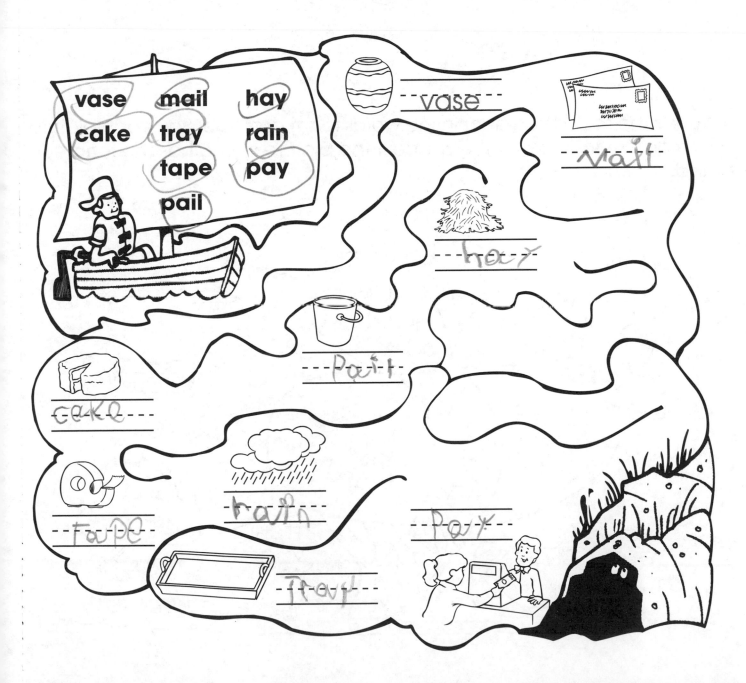

Long Vowel e

What does the t**ea**m s**ee** in the tr**ee**?

team   **tree**

Long e is the sound you hear in the words **team** and **tree**. Say each picture name on the tree. **Color** the space if the picture name has the **long e** sound.

Long Vowel e

Take a s<u>ea</u>t in the j<u>ee</u>p.

Long e is the sound you hear in the words **seat** and **jeep**. Take a ride in the jeep to see an animal that is the symbol of the United States. **Draw** a line to follow the path that has the **long e** words to find out which animal it is.

heel   meat

bee   wet

hen

read   pet

time   ten   mail

keep   team

dig   sail   see   tie

week

Long Vowel e

Read each sentence. **Circle** the word that completes each sentence.
Write the word on the line.

1. We all help make the _____ .

   feet   eat   meal

2. Dad heats the _____ .

   beef   mean   read

3. Lee cleans the green _____ leak _____ .

   beaks   leak   beans

4. Mom has an orange to _____ .

   peas   peel   pail

5. I will take a _____ .

   poke   jeep   peek

Long Vowel i
Mike will dive for a dime.

 **dime**

Long i is the sound you hear in the word **dime**. Mike dives only for things whose names have the **long i** sound. **Circle** the things Mike will dive for.

Long Vowel i

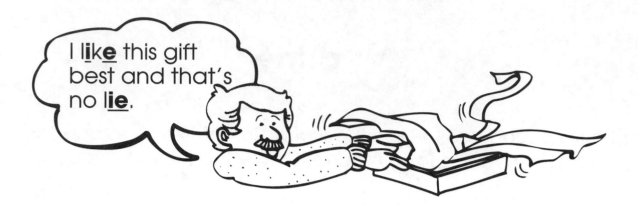

I l**i**k**e** this gift best and that's no l**ie**.

Long i is the sound you hear in the words **like** and **lie**. Read each word below. Find out what gift Dad likes best by **coloring** the spaces with the **long i** sound.

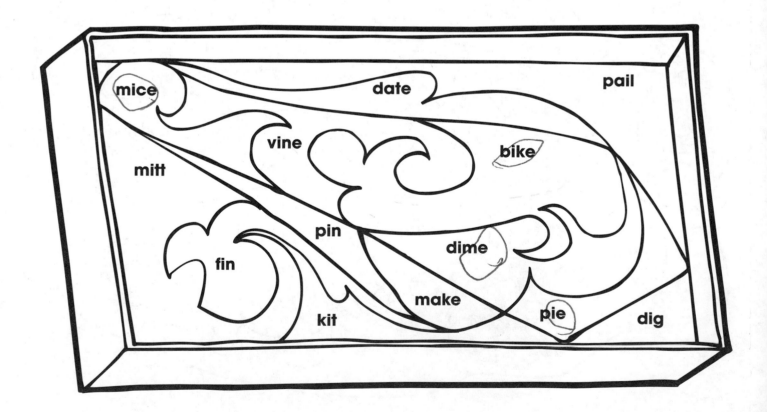

Long Vowel i

Words that have the same ending sounds are called **rhyming words**. Read the words on each kite. **Color** the kites that have three rhyming **long i** words.

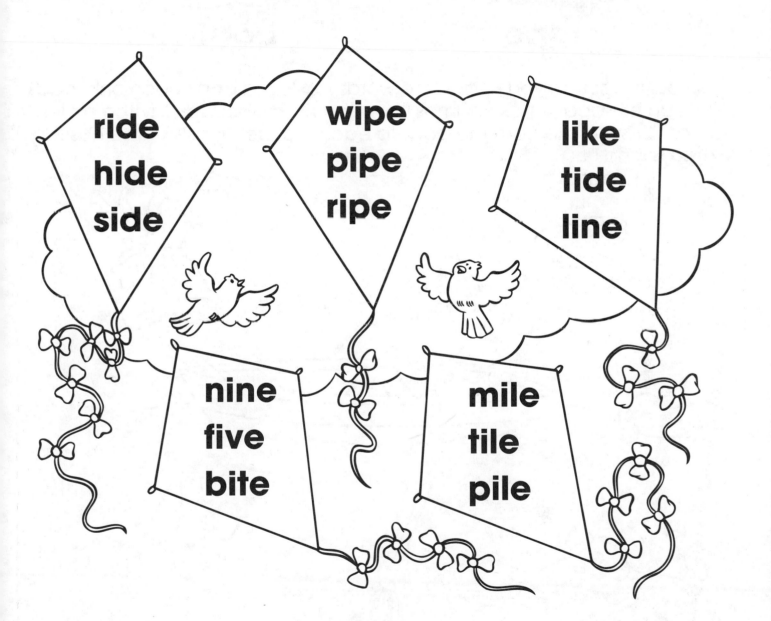

ride
hide
side

wipe
pipe
ripe

like
tide
line

nine
five
bite

mile
tile
pile

Long Vowel o

J**oa**n l**oa**ds a r**o**p**e** on her b**oa**t.

rope

boat

Long o is the sound you hear in the words **rope** and **boat**. Joan only loads things on her boat whose names have the **long o** sound. Say the picture names. **Draw** a line from the boat to each picture whose name has the **long o** sound.

Long Vowel o

J**oe** used a c**oa**t, a b**ow** and a carrot for the n**os**e.

Long o is the sound you hear in the words **Joe**, **coat**, **bow** and **nose**. **Cut out** the flash cards. Sort them by different spellings for the sound of **long o**. Read each word. Then, **make up** a game to play with the cards.

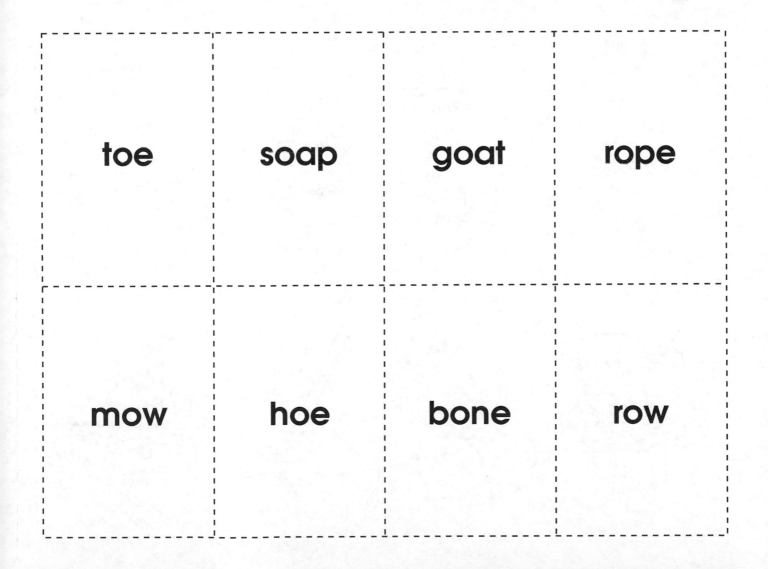

toe	soap	goat	rope
mow	hoe	bone	row

Long Vowel o

Long Vowel o

Say the name of each picture. Finish the name by **writing o** and **e** or **oa** when you hear the **long o** sound.

b o n e   t o p   c o n e

f r o g   c o t   g o a t

f o x   n o s e   r o p e

Long Vowel u
The c<u>u</u>t<u>e</u> cub sits on a c<u>u</u>b<u>e</u>.

 **cube**

Long u is the sound you hear in the word **cube**. **Cut out** the pictures at the bottom. Say each picture name. **Glue** the pictures on the cube whose names have the **long u** sound.

Long Vowel u
The c**ute** m**ule** pulls a cart to the village.

Long u is the sound you hear in the words **cute** and **mule**. Read the words at the bottom of the page. **Draw** a picture to go with each **long u** word.

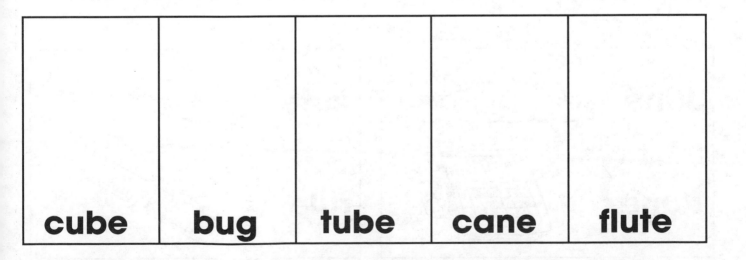

| cube | bug | tube | cane | flute |

Long Vowel u

Look at the pictures. Read the words. **Draw** a line from each word to its picture.

cute

cube

prune

tune

mule

huge

fuse

tube

June

dune

flute

rule

GREAT JOB!

COOL!

Fantastic!

WOW!

WAY TO GO!

Long Vowels

Write **a**, **e**, **i**, **o** or **u** in each blank to complete the word. **Draw** a line from the word to its picture.

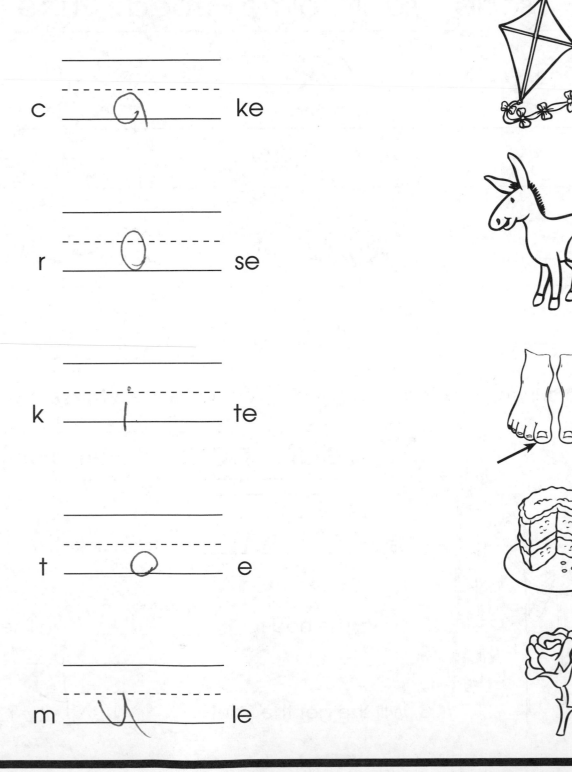

c _____a_____ ke

r _____o_____ se

k _____i_____ te

t _____o_____ e

m _____u_____ le

Long Vowels

Read the words in the box. Use the words to write the name of each picture. **Write** the name on the line.

| rain | soap | seal | dime | toad | tube |

soap

dime

toad

rain

tube

seal

Find the word in the box that completes each sentence. **Write** the word on the line.

| seat | paid | wait |

1. Jean __paid__ for a ticket.

2. Then, she had to __wait__ in line.

3. Will she get the front __seat__?

The Super Silent E

cap + e = cape

Adding **e** to the end of the **short vowel** word **cap** changes it to the **long vowel** word **cape**. **Cut out** the tub. **Cut on** the dotted lines to make slits. **Slip** the water through the slits in the tub. Next, **cut out** the tube. **Glue** the tube in the tub, but don't glue the cap down. When the cap is on the tube, read the short vowel word. Then, **fold** the cap back to show the **e**. Read the long vowel word.

Example:

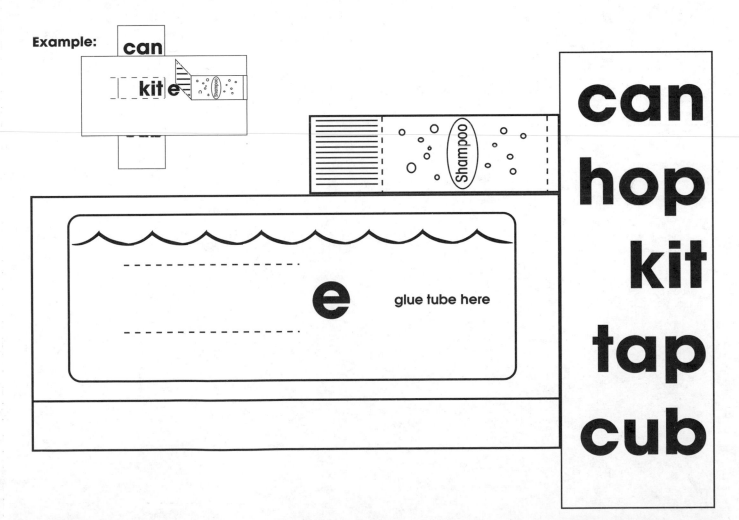

glue tube here

can
hop
kit
tap
cub

Page is blank for cutting exercise on previous page.

The Super Silent E

When you add an **e** to the end of some words, the vowel changes from a short vowel sound to a long vowel sound.

Example: rip + **e** = ripe.

Say the word under the first picture in each pair. Then, **add** an **e** to the word under the matching picture. Say the new word.

pet + e = _Pete_

tub + e = _tube_

man + e _mane_

kit + e = _kite_

pin + e = _pine_

cap + e = _cape_

Words With Super Silent E

When a **Super Silent E** appears at the end of a word, you can't hear it, but it makes the other vowel have a **long** sound. For example, **tub** has a **short** vowel sound, and **tube** has a **long** vowel sound.

Look at the following pictures. Decide if the word has a short or long vowel sound. **Circle** the correct word. Watch for the **Super Silent E!**

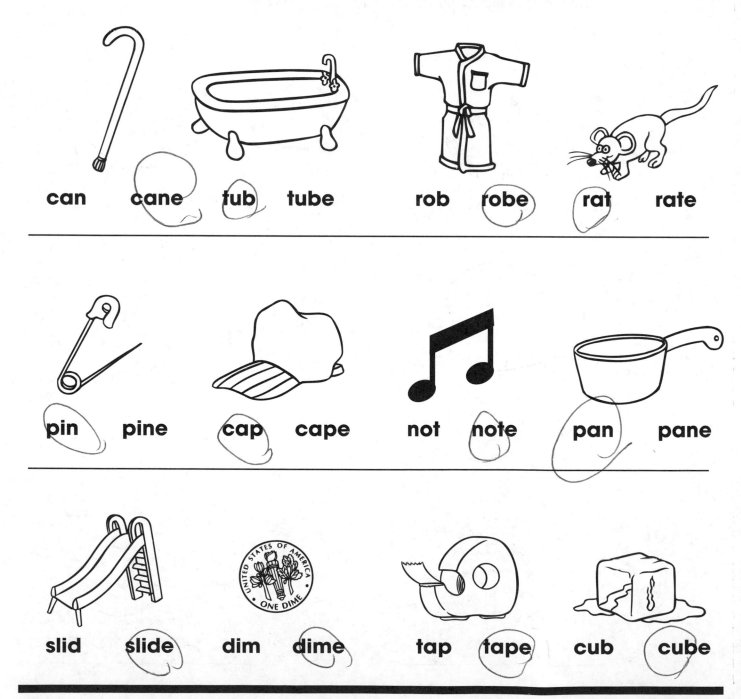

can   cane   tub   tube   rob   robe   rat   rate

pin   pine   cap   cape   not   note   pan   pane

slid   slide   dim   dime   tap   tape   cub   cube

Final y as a Vowel

Our pupp**y** stays dr**y** in the yard.

You know that **y** is a consonant. When **y** is at the beginning of a word, it makes the sound at the beginning of **yard**.

Y can also be a vowel.

Sometimes **y** can have the **long e** sound you hear at the end of **puppy**. **Y** has this sound when it is at the end of a word with more than one syllable or part.

Sometimes **y** can have the **long i** sound you hear at the end of **dry**. **Y** has this sound when it is at the end of a one-syllable word.

Say each picture name. **Circle** the word that names the picture. If **y** makes the **long e** sound, **color** the picture **brown**. If **y** makes the **long i** sound, **color** the picture **orange**.

bail
bay
baby

crazy
cry
crate

bunt
bunny
buy

fry
frosty
frog

pay
pry
pony

fly
feed
fussy

y as a Vowel

Y at the end of a word is a vowel. When **y** is at the end of a one-syllable word, it has the sound of a **long i** (as in **my**). When **y** is at the end of a word with more than one syllable, it has the sound of a **long e** (as in **baby**). Look at the words in the box. If the word has the sound of a **long i**, write it under the word **my**. If the word has the sound of a **long e**, write it under the word **baby**. **Write** the word from the box that answers each riddle.

| happy | penny | try | sleepy | dry |
| bunny | why | sky | party | fly |

my   **baby**

_____   _____

_____   _____

_____   _____

_____   _____

1. It takes five of these to make a nickel.   _____

2. This is what you call a baby rabbit.   _____

3. It is often blue and you can see it if you look up.   _____

4. You might have one of these on your birthday.   _____

5. It is the opposite of wet.   _____

6. You might use this word to ask a question.   _____

7. This is what birds and airplanes can do.   _____

Vowel Teams au, aw, oo

These vowel teams put two vowels together to make one new sound. Look at the first picture in each row. **Circle** the things that have the same sound.

faucet

saw

boots

cook

Vowel Teams oi, oy, ou, ow

These vowel teams put two vowels together to make one new sound. Look at the first picture in each row. **Circle** the things that have the same sound.

oil

toy

couch

howl

Vowel Teams ou and ow, au and aw

The vowel teams **ou** and **ow** can have the same sound. You can hear it in the words **clown** and **cloud**. The vowel teams **au** and **aw** have the same sound. You hear it in the words **because** and **law**.

Look at the pictures. **Write** the correct vowel team to complete the words. The first one is done for you.

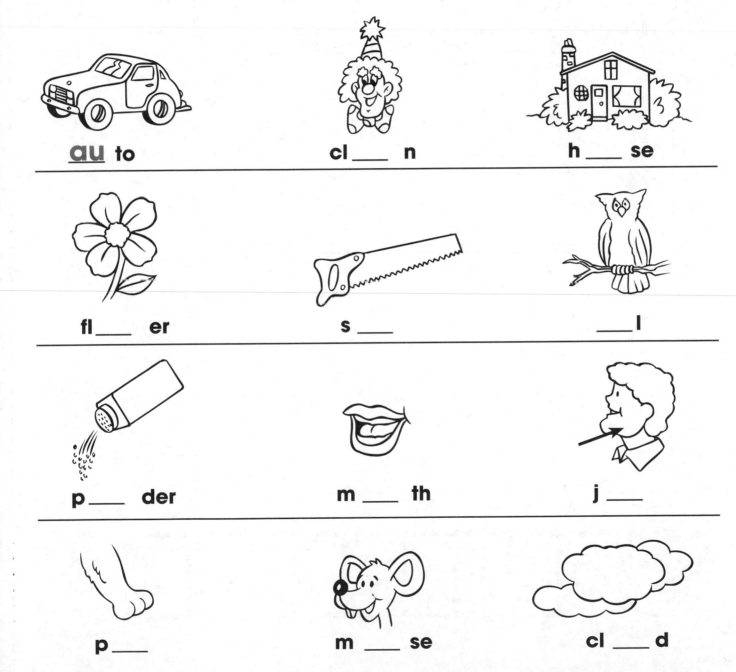

<u>au</u> to

cl ___ n

h ___ se

fl ___ er

s ___

___ l

p ___ der

m ___ th

j ___

p ___

m ___ se

cl ___ d

Today is a beautiful day.

Learning is fun!

What have you learned today?

SENTENCES

Matching Pictures and Sentences

Sentences can tell us something. **Draw** a line from the picture to the sentence that tells about it.

Kelly has flowers in her basket.

An apple is on the tree.

Four ducks swim in the lake.

The toy train goes fast!

The brown bear is eating honey.

Telling Sentences

Telling sentences begin with a **capital letter**. They end with a **period**.

Read the sentences. **Draw** a **yellow circle** around the **capital letter** at the beginning of the sentence. **Draw** a **purple circle** around the **period** at the end of the sentence.

1. I am seven years old.

2. The bird is pretty.

3. The boy likes to dance.

4. Turtles like to swim.

Telling Sentences

Read the sentences. Write them below. **Begin** each sentence with a **capital letter** and end it with a **period**.

1. i like to go to the store with Mom

2. we go on Friday

3. i get to push the cart

4. i like to help Mom

1. _____

2. _____

3. _____

4. _____

Telling Sentences

A sentence tells a complete idea.

Circle the group of words if it tells a complete idea.

1. Grass is a green plant.

2. Mowing the lawn.

3. Grass grows in fields and lawns.

4. Tickle the feet.

5. Sheep, cows and horses eat grass.

6. We like to play in.

7. My sister likes to mow the lawn.

8. A picnic on the grass.

9. My dog likes to roll in the grass.

10. Plant flowers around.

Telling Sentences

Circle the group of words if it tells a complete idea.

1. A secret is something you know.

2. Mom's birthday gift is a secret.

3. Something nobody knows.

4. If you promise not to.

5. I'll tell you a secret.

6. No one else.

Asking Sentences

Asking sentences ask a question. An asking sentence begins with a **capital letter**. It ends with a **question mark**. **Draw** a **blue line** under the sentences that ask a question.

1. We like to camp.

2. We like to sing at camp.

3. We like to cook hot dogs.

4. We like to sleep in a tent.

5. Do you like to camp?

6. Can you make a fire?

Asking Sentences

Asking sentences are also called **questions**. **Copy** the questions on the line below. **Begin** each sentence with a capital letter and end it with a question mark.

1. will you be my friend

_____

- -

_____

2. what is your name

_____

- -

_____

3. are you eight-years-old

_____

- -

_____

4. do you like rainbows

_____

- -

_____

Periods and Question Marks

Use a period at the end of a telling sentence. Use a question mark at the end of an asking sentence.

Put a period or a question mark at the end of each sentence below.

1. Do you like a parade

2. The balloons are big

3. The clowns lead the parade

4. Can you see the horses

Surprising Sentences

Some sentences tell a strong feeling and end with an **exclamation mark (!)**. A surprising sentence may be only one or two words showing fear, surprise or pain, such as "Oh, no!"

Put a **period** at the end of the sentences that tell something. **Put** an **exclamation mark** at the end of the sentences that tell a strong feeling. **Put** a **question mark** at the end of the sentences that ask a question.

1. The cheetah can run very fast

2. Wow

3. Look at that cheetah go

4. Can you run fast

5. Oh, my

6. You're faster than I am

7. Let's run together

8. We can run as fast as a cheetah

9. What fun

10. Do you think cheetahs get tired

Commands

Commands tell someone to do something. "Be careful." is a command. It can also be written as "Be careful!" with an exclamation point if it tells a strong feeling.

Put a period at the end of each command sentence. **Use** an exclamation point if the sentence tells a strong feeling. Then, **write** your own commands on the lines below.

1. Clean your room

2. Now

3. Be careful with your goldfish

4. Watch out

5. Be a little more careful

6. Take your books with you

1. _____

2. _____

Sentences

A **story** has more than one sentence. **Use** the words from the pictures to write a story.

girl

boy

play

books   swing   school

I am a happy _____ . I go to _____ .

I like to read _____ . I like to _____

on the playground. I like to _____ on the swings.

Sentences

Draw a picture of yourself in the box marked **Me**. Then, **write** three sentences about yourself on the lines.

Me

1. _____

2. _____

3. _____

COMPREHENSION

Boats

Read about boats. Then, **answer** the questions.

See the boats! They float on water. Some boats have sails. The wind moves the sails. It makes the boats go. Many people name their sailboats. They paint the name on the side of the boat.

1. What makes sailboats move? _____

2. Where do sailboats float? _____

3. What would you name a sailboat? _____

Tigers

Read about tigers. Then, answer the questions.

Tigers sleep during the day. They hunt at night. Tigers eat meat. They hunt deer. They like to eat wild pigs. If they cannot find meat on land, tigers will eat fish.

1. When do tigers sleep?   night   day

2. Name two things tigers eat.

_____   _____

\- - - - - - - - - - - - - - - - -   - - - - - - - - - - - - - - - - -

_____   _____

3. When do tigers hunt?   day   night

Where Flowers Grow

Read about flowers. Then, **answer** the questions.

Some flowers grow in pots. Many flowers grow in flower beds. Others grow beside the road. Some flowers begin from seeds. They grow into small buds. Then, they open wide and bloom. Flowers are pretty!

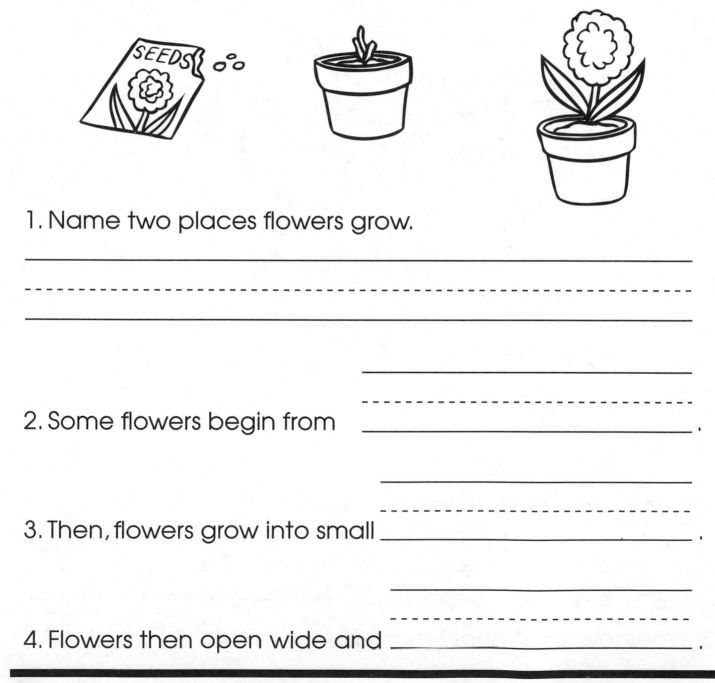

1. Name two places flowers grow.

_____

- -

_____

2. Some flowers begin from _____.

3. Then, flowers grow into small _____.

4. Flowers then open wide and _____.

Fish Come In Many Colors

Read about the color of fish. Then, tell the colors and **color** the fish.

   All fish live in water. Fish that live at the top are blue, green or black. Fish that live down deep are silver or red. The colors make it hard to see the fish.

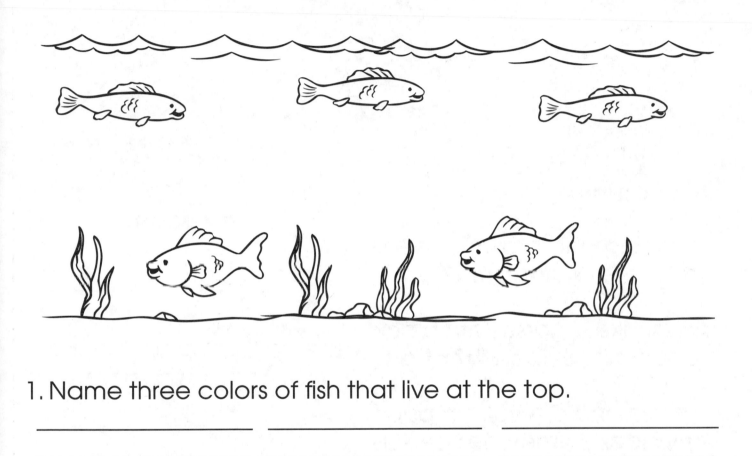

1. Name three colors of fish that live at the top.

_____   _____   _____

_____   _____   _____

2. Name two colors of fish that live down deep.

_____   _____

_____   _____

3. Color the top fish and the bottom fish the correct colors.

Zoo Animal Riddles

Write the name of the animal that answers each riddle.

bear

zebra

lion

camel

elephant

1. I am big and brown. I sleep all winter. **What am I?**

   _____

2. I look like a horse with black and white stripes. **What am I?**

   _____

3. I have one or two humps on my back. Sometimes people ride on me. **What am I?**

   _____

4. I am a very big animal. I have a long nose called a trunk. **What am I?**

   _____

5. I have sharp claws and teeth. I am a great big cat. **What am I?** _____

Nursery Rhyme Riddles

Write the name of the character to answer each riddle.

Little Bo Peep

Little Jack Horner

Wee Willie Winkie

Little Red Riding Hood

Little Miss Muffet

1. A spider frightened me! **Who am I?**

   _____

2. You will find me in a corner eating pie.

   Who am I? _____

3. A wolf scared me while I was on my way to Grandmother's!

   Who am I? _____

4. I've lost my sheep. **Who am I?** _____

5. I ran through the town in my nightgown.

   Who am I? _____

Important Signs To Know

Draw a line from the sign to the sentence that tells about it.

1. If you see this sign, watch out for trains.

2. When cars or bikes come to this sign, they must stop.

3. When this sign is on, do not cross the street.

4. This sign tells you to stay out of the yard.

5. If you see this sign, do not eat or drink what is inside!

6. This sign warns you that it is not safe. Stay away!

7. This sign says you are not allowed to come in.

Sequencing

Look at the picture story. Read the sentences. Then, **write 1, 2, 3** or **4** by each sentence to show the order of the story.

Ben rides the bus._____

Ben is at the bus stop._____

Ben leaves his house._____

Ben gets on the bus._____

Comprehension: Sequencing

Kate is sick. What do you think happened? **Put** numbers beside each sentence to tell the story.

_____ She went to the doctor's office.

_____ Kate felt much better.

_____ Kate felt very hot and tired.

_____ Kate's mother went to the drug store.

_____ The doctor looked in Kate's ears.

_____ Kate took a pill.

_____ The doctor gave Kate's mother a piece of paper.

Sequencing

Tom and Tess are making a snack. They are fixing nacho chips and cheese.

Look at the picture. Then, look at the steps that Tom and Tess use. **Put** numbers beside each sentence to tell the correct order. Then, **color** the picture.

_____ Tom and Tess cook the chips in the microwave oven for 2 minutes.

_____ They get out a plate to cook on.

_____ Tom and Tess get out the nacho chips and cheese.

_____ Tom and Tess eat the food.

_____ They put the chips on a plate.

_____ They put cheese on the chips.

Following Directions

Read the sentences. Follow the directions.

Bob is making a snowman. He needs your help. **Draw** a **black hat** on the snowman. **Draw red buttons**. Now, **draw** a **green scarf**. **Draw** a **happy face** on the snowman.

Following Directions

Follow the directions to make a paper sack puppet.

Find a small sack that fits your hand. Make a face where the sack folds. Cut out teeth from colored paper. Glue them on the sack. Cut out ears. Cut out a nose. Cut out a mouth. Glue them all on.

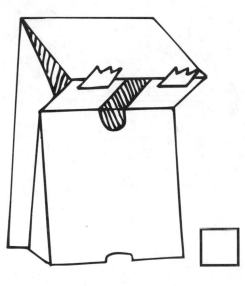

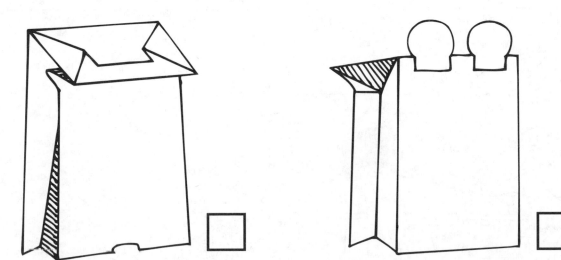

Number the pictures **1**, **2**, **3** and **4** to show the correct order.

Predicting Outcome

Read the story. Use the last box to finish it. Then, **color** the pictures.

1. "Look at that elephant! He sure is big!"

2. "I'm hungry."
   "I'll bet that elephant is, too."

3. "Stop, Tess! Look at that sign!"

Don't Feed the Animals

4. What will Tom and Tess do?

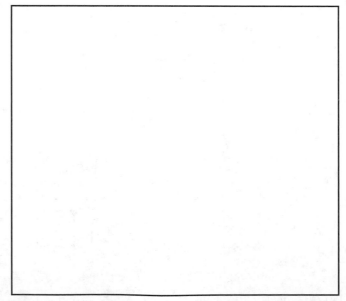

Predicting Outcome

Read the story. Finish the story the way you think it should end. Then, **color** the pictures.

1. A cat is playing with a ball of yarn.

2. A mouse begins peeking around the corner.

3. The mouse tiptoes past the playful cat.

4. What do you think will happen?

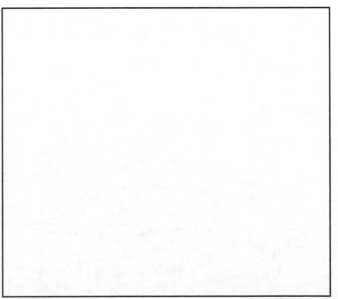

Predicting Outcomes

Read the story. Then, **follow** the instructions.

Ben and Ann were washing Spot. His fur was wet. Their hands were wet. Spot did NOT like to be wet. Ben dropped the soap. Ann picked it up and let go of Spot. Uh-oh!

1. **Write** what happened next.

_____

- -

_____

- -

_____

2. **Draw** what happened next.

Making Inferences

Read the story. Then, **answer** the questions.

Mrs. Posey is looking forward to a visit from Grandma Dapper. In the morning, she cleans her house. She bakes a cherry pie. An hour before Grandma Dapper is to arrive, the phone rings. Mrs. Posey says she understands. But she looks very sad.

1. Who do you think called Mrs. Posey?

_____

- -

_____

2. Why is Mrs. Posey sad?

_____

- -

_____

Making Inferences

Read the story. Then, **answer** the questions.

Tom is baking cookies. He wears special clothes when he bakes. He puts flour, sugar, eggs and butter into a bowl. He mixes everything together. He puts the cookies in the oven at 11:15 a.m. It takes them 15 minutes to bake. Tom wants something cold and white to drink when he eats his cookies.

1. Tom is baking a cake. **True** or **False**   (Circle one.)

2. Tom wears a (**hat   mittens   apron   tie**) when he bakes. (Circle two.)

3. **Cross out** the thing Tom **does not** put in the cookies.

    flour   eggs   milk   butter   sugar

4. What time will the cookies be done? _____

5. What will Tom drink with his cookies? _____

Making Inferences

Read the story. Then, **follow** the instructions.

John and his dad are going to a baseball game today. The game starts at 2:00 p.m. John wakes up at 9:00 a.m. He has a swimming class at 10:30. His class is over at 11:30 a.m. John has lunch at noon. Then, he must clean his room. Dad says, "We must leave at 1:30." But John wants to play with his friend, too. Dad says, "Play after you clean your room, but before we leave for the game."

1. Use a **black crayon** to draw the game time on the clock.

2. Use a **red crayon** to draw when swimming class starts.

3. How long is swimming class? _____

4. Use an **orange crayon** to draw lunch time on the clock.

5. Use a **blue crayon** to draw the time when John and his dad must leave for the game.

Main Idea

The **main idea** of a story is what the story is mostly about. Read the story about jokes. Then, **follow** the directions.

Most kids like jokes. Some jokes are very long. Some jokes are short. Good jokes are funny. Do you know a funny joke?

Circle one. The main idea of this story is:
There are many kinds of jokes.   Some jokes are short.

Here is a joke for you to finish! What did the rug say to

_____

- -

_____

Main Idea

Read the story. Then, **answer** the questions.

It is cold in the winter. Snow falls. Water freezes. Most kids like to play outdoors. Some kids make a snowman. Some kids skate. What do you do in winter?

1. Circle one. The main idea is:

| Snow falls in the winter. | In winter, there are many things to do outside. |

2. Tell 2 things about winter weather.

_____

- -

_____

- -

_____

3. Tell what you like to do in winter.

- -

_____

Making Deductions

Tom and Tess are late for dinner. What time is dinner?

Look at the clock. Then, **answer** the questions.

1. It is now 6:00 p.m. Use an
   orange crayon for the clock's hands.

2. It was 3:00 when they left home.
   Draw the clock hands in **blue**.

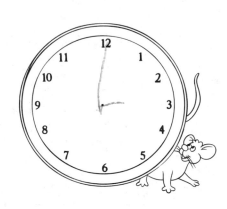

3. Mother said, "Dinner is in two hours. Be home then."
   Draw the clock hands in **purple.**

4. What time were they to be home?

   _____

Making Deductions

Use the clues to help the children find their books. **Draw** a line from each child's name to the correct book.

Clues

1. John likes to make people laugh.

2. Lola likes to bake.

3. Bill likes faraway places.

4. Tess does not like monsters or flags.

5. Jim does not like space or monsters.

6. Tom does not like games, jokes or cakes.

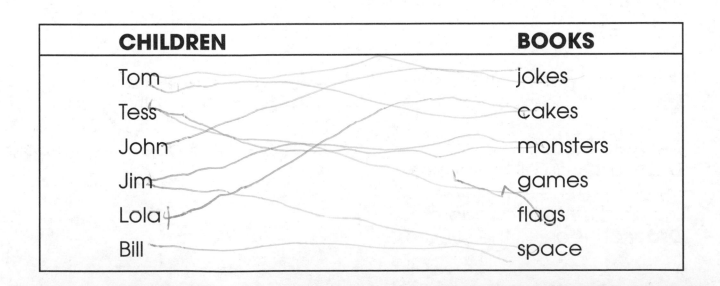

CHILDREN	BOOKS
Tom	jokes
Tess	cakes
John	monsters
Jim	games
Lola	flags
Bill	space

Making Deductions

Tom and Tess are looking for gold. They have found many shapes. Which one has gold in it?

Look at the shapes. Then, **answer** the questions.

1. The gold is **not** in a triangle.
   Draw an **X** on all the triangles.

2. The gold is **not** in a circle.
   Draw an **X** on all the circles.

3. The gold is **not** in a square.
   Draw an **X** on all the squares.

4. The gold is **not** in a star.
   Draw an **X** on all the stars.

5. **Circle** the shape with the gold.

Making Deductions

Dad is cooking dinner tonight.

Look at the clues below. **Fill in** the menu. What day is it?

MENU	
Sunday	_____
Monday	_____
Tuesday	_____
Wednesday	_____
Thursday	_____
Friday	_____
Saturday	_____

Clues

1. Mom fixed pizza on Monday.
2. Dad fixed cheese rolls the day before that.
3. Tess made a potpie three days after Mom fixed pizza.
4. Tom fixed corn-on-the-cob the day before Tess made potpie.
5. Mom fixed hot dogs the day after Tess made the potpie.
6. Tess cooked fish the day before Dad fixed cheese rolls.
7. Dad is making chicken today. What day is it? _____

LANGUAGE SKILLS

Nouns

Nouns tell the name of a person, place or thing.

Look at each picture. **Color** it **red** if it names a **person**. **Color** it **blue** if it names a **place**. **Color** it **green** if it names a **thing**.

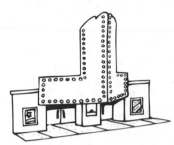
movie theater

grandfather

dinosaur

flower

park

girl

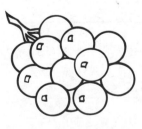
grapes

fireman

library

Nouns

Write these naming words next to the correct pictures below.

| store | zoo | child | baby | teacher | table |
| cat | park | gym | woman | sock | horse |

Person

child, women, baby
tecner

Place

Gym   Store
Park   Zoo

Thing

table   horse
sock   cat

Nouns

The name of a person, place or thing is a noun.

Read the story and **circle** all the nouns. Then, **write** the nouns next to the pictures below.

Our family likes to go to the park.

_____

We play on the swings.

_____

We eat cake.

_____

We drink lemonade.

_____

We throw the ball to our dog.

_____

Nouns

We begin the names of people, places and pets with a capital letter.

Write the names on the lines below. Use capital letters at the beginning of each word.

spot

mike smith

washington, d.c.

fluffy

lynn cramer

buster

Pronouns

Sometimes we use other words to name people: for a boy or a man, we use **he**. For a girl or a woman, we use **she**. For two or more people, we use **they**. **He**, **she** and **they** are called **pronouns**.

Write he, she or **they** in these sentences. The first one shows you what to do.

The boy likes cookies.

He likes cookies.

1. The girl is running fast.

She is running fast.

2. The man reads the paper.

He reads the paper.

3. The woman has a cold.

She has a cold.

4. Two children came to school.

They came to school.

Pronouns

Pronouns are words that can be used instead of nouns. **She**, **he**, **it** and **they** are pronouns.

Read the sentence. Then, **write** the sentence again, using a pronoun in the blank.

She   He   It   They

1. Dan likes funny jokes. _____ likes funny jokes.

2. Peg and Sam went to the zoo. _____ went to the zoo.

3. My dog likes to dig in the yard. _____ likes to dig in the yard.

4. Sara is a very good dancer. _____ is a very good dancer.

5. Fred and Ed are twins. _____ are twins.

Verbs

Verbs are words that tell what a person or thing can do.

Look at the pictures. Read the words. **Write** a verb in each sentence below.

1. The two boys like to _____ together.

2. The children _____ the soccer ball.

3. Some children like to _____ _swing_ _____ on the swings.

4. The girl can _____ very fast.

5. The teacher will _____ the bell.

Verbs

A **verb** is the **action word** in a sentence. **Run**, **sleep** and **jump** are verbs.

Circle the verbs in the sentence below.

1. We play baseball every day.

2. We go to the field after school.

3. Susan pitches the ball very well.

4. Mike swings the bat hard.

5. Chris runs to home base.

6. Laura hits a home run.

Language Skills

Verbs

We use verbs to tell when something happens. Sometimes we add **ed** to verbs to tell us if something has already happened.

Example: Today, we play. Yesterday, we play**ed**.

Write the correct verb in the blank.

1. Today I will _____ my dog, Fritz.
   wash   washed

2. Last week, Fritz _____ when we said, "Bath time, Fritz."
   cry   cried

3. My sister likes to _____ wash Fritz.
   help   helped

4. One time, she _____ Fritz by herself.
   clean   cleaned

5. Fritz will _____ a lot better after his bath.
   look   looked

Nouns and Verbs

Read the sentences below. **Draw** a **circle** around the nouns. **Underline** the verbs.

Example: (John) drinks juice every morning.

1. Our class skates at the roller-skating rink.

2. We go after school on Fridays.

3. Mike and Jan go very fast.

4. Fred eats hot dogs.

5. Sue dances to the music.

6. Everyone likes the skating rink.

Nouns and Verbs

Read the sentences below. **Draw** a **circle** around the nouns. **Underline** the verbs.

1. The boy runs fast.

2. The turtle eats leaves.

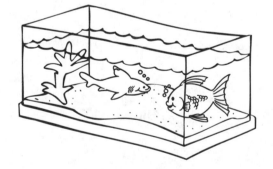

3. The fish swim in the tank.

4. The girl hits the ball.

Parts of a Sentence

Look at the pictures. **Match** a naming part to an action part to make a sentence that tells about the picture.

The boy   delivered the mail.

A small dog   threw a football.

The mailman   fell down.

The goalie   chased the ball.

More Than One

Some nouns name more than one person, place or thing.

Add **s** to make the words tell about the picture.

frog____

pan ____

boy ____

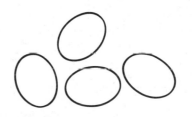
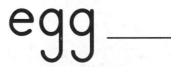

egg____

horn ____

girl____

More Than One

An **s** at the end of a word often means there is more than one. Words that mean more than one are also called **plurals**.

Look at each picture and **circle** the correct word. **Write** the word on the line.

two

dog   dogs

_____

- - - - - - - - - - - - - - - - - -

_____

four

flower   flowers

_____

- - - - - - - - - - - - - - - - - -

_____

one

bikes   bike

_____

- - - - - - - - - - - - - - - - - -

_____

three

toys   toy

_____

- - - - - - - - - - - - - - - - - -

_____

a

lamb   lambs

_____

- - - - - - - - - - - - - - - - - -

_____

two

cat   cats

_____

- - - - - - - - - - - - - - - - - -

_____

More Than One

To show two or more of something, we add **s** to most words.

    one dog - **two dogs**   one book - **two books**

For words that end with **x**, use **es** to show more than one.

    one fox - **two foxes**   one box - **two boxes**

The spelling of some words change when there are more than one.

    one mouse - **two mice**

Some words stay the same, even when there are more than one of something.

    one deer - **two deer**   one fish - **two fish**

Finish the sentences with the correct words.

1. The _____ run fast.

2. The _____ are eating.

3. Have you seen any _____ today?

4. Where do the _____ live?

5. Did you ever have _____ for pets?

More Than One

To make a word mean more than one, you usually add an **s** or **es** to the word. Some words ending in **y** change the **y** to an **i** before adding **es**. For example, **baby** changes to **babies**.

Look at the following lists of words. **Write** the plural form of the word next to it. The first one shows you what to do.

fox   foxes _____

bush _____

class _____

chair _____

shoe _____

story _____

puppy _____

match _____

car _____

ball _____

candy _____

wish _____

box _____

lady _____

bunny _____

desk _____

dish _____

pencil _____

Is and Are

Is and **are** are special action words. Use the word **is** when talking about one person or thing. Use the word **are** when talking about more than one person, place or thing.

Example: The dog **is** barking.
The dogs **are** barking.

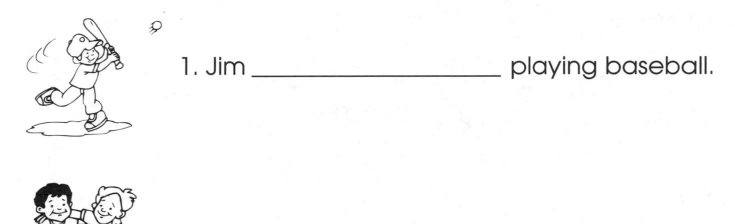

1. Jim _____ playing baseball.

2. Fred and Sam _____ good friends.

3. Cupcakes _____ my favorite treat.

4. Lisa _____ a good soccer player.

Is, Are and Am

Is, **are** and **am** are special action words that tell us something is happening now.

We use **am** with **I**. **Example:** I **am** eating breakfast.

We use **is** to tell about one person or thing. **Example:** He **is** eating breakfast.

We use **are** to tell about more than one. **Example:** We **are** eating breakfast.

We use **are** with **you**. **Example:** You **are** eating breakfast.

Write is, **are** or **am** in the sentences below.

1. My friends _____ helping me build a tree house.

2. It _____ in my backyard.

3. We _____ using hammers, wood and nails.

4. It _____ a very hard job.

5. I _____ lucky to have good friends.

Was and Were

Was and **were** are action words that tell us something has already happened.

Use **was** to tell about one person or thing. **Example:** I **was** coming to your house.

Use **were** to tell about more than one person, place or thing or when using the word **you**. **Example:** We **were** coming to your house.

Write was or **were** in each sentence.

1. Lily _____ eight-years-old on her birthday.

2. Tim and Steve _____ happy to be at the party.

3. Megan _____ too shy to sing "Happy Birthday."

4. Ben _____ sorry he dropped his cake.

5. All of the children _____ happy to be invited.

Ownership

We add **'s** to nouns (people, places or things) to tell who or what owns something.

Read the sentences. **Fill in** the blanks to show ownership. **Write** the sentences to show ownership.

Example: The doll belongs to Sara.

It is ___Sara's___ doll.

1. Sparky has a red collar.

_____

_____ collar is red.

2. Jimmy has a blue coat.

_____

_____ coat is blue.

3. The tail of the cat is short.

_____

The _____ tail is short.

Ownership

Read the sentences. **Choose** the correct word and **write** it in the sentences below.

1. The _____*boys*_____ lunchbox is broken.
    boys   boy's

2. The _____*gerdils*_____ are sleeping.
    gerbil's   gerbils

3. _____*Anns*_____ hair is brown.
    Anns   Ann's

4. The _____*horses*_____ run fast.
    horse's   horses

5. My _____*sisters*_____ coat is torn.
    sister's   sisters

6. The _____*Monkeys*_____ were playing.
    monkeys   monkey's

7. The _____*Birds*_____ wing is broken.
    birds   bird's

8. The _____*dogs*_____ paws are muddy.
    dogs   dog's

Words That Describe

Describing words tell us more about a person, place or thing.

Read the words in the box. **Choose** a word that describes the picture. **Write** it next to the picture.

| happy | round | sick | cold | long |

long

happy

sick

round

cold

Adjectives

Describing words are also called **adjectives**.

Circle the describing words in the sentences.

1. The juicy apple is on the plate.

2. The furry dog is eating a bone.

3. It was a sunny day.

4. The kitten drinks warm milk.

5. The baby has a loud cry.

Adjectives

Think of your own describing words. Write a story about Smokey, the cat.

Smokey is a _____ cat. His fur is _____ .

He likes to chew on my _____ shoes. He likes to

eat _____ cat food. I like Smokey because he

is so _____ .

Articles

Articles are small words that help us better understand nouns. **A** and **an** are articles. We use **an** before a word that begins with a vowel. We use **a** before a word that begins with a consonant.

Example: We looked in **a** nest. It had **an** eagle in it.

1. I found _____ book.

2. It had a story about _____ ant in it.

3. In the story, _____ lion gave three wishes to _____ ant.

4. The ant's first wish was to ride _____ elephant.

5. The second wish was to ride _____ alligator.

6. The last wish was _____ wish for three more wishes.

Suffixes

A suffix is a syllable added to the end of a word which changes its meaning as in small, small**er** and small**est**. The word you start with is called the **root word**. Some root words change their spelling before adding **er** and **est**. For example, in the word **big** another **g** is added to make the words big**ger** and big**gest**. In the word pretty, the **y** changes to an **i** to make the words prett**ier** and prett**iest**.

Use words from the box to help you add **er** and **est** to the root words.

prettier	happier	luckiest	busiest	tinier
luckier	silliest	busier	prettiest	funnier
tiniest	happiest	bigger	biggest	sillier
funniest				

	er	**est**
happy	_____	_____
busy	_____	_____
tiny	_____	_____
pretty	_____	_____
lucky	_____	_____
big	_____	_____
silly	_____	_____
funny	_____	_____

Suffixes

Adding **ing** to a word means that it is happening now. Adding **ed** to a word means it happened in the past.

Look at the words in the box. **Underline** the root word in each one. **Write** the word from the box that completes each sentence.

snowing	wished	played	looking
crying	walked	eating	going

1. We like to play. We _____ yesterday.

2. Is that snow? Yes, it is _____ .

3. Do you want to go with me? No, I am _____ with my friend.

4. The baby will cry if we leave. The baby is _____ .

5. We will walk home from school. We_____ to school this morning.

6. Did you wish for a new bike? Yes, I _____ for one.

7. Will you look at the book? I am _____ at it now.

8. I hope we eat early today. We are _____ pizza today.

Suffixes

Add the suffixes to the root word to make new words. Use your new words to complete the sentences.

help + ful = _____

care + less = _____

build + er = _____

talk + ed = _____

love + ly = _____

loud + er = _____

1. My mother _____ to my teacher about my homework.

2. The radio was _____ than the television.

3. Sally is always _____ to her mother.

4. A _____ put a new garage on our house.

5. The flowers are _____ .

6. It is _____ to cross the street without looking both ways.

Prefixes

A prefix is a syllable added to the beginning of a word which changes it? meaning.

Read the prefix and its meaning. Add the prefix to the root word to make a new word. **Finish** the sentences using the new words.

Prefixes	(Meaning)	Root Word	New Word
bi	(two)	cycle	_____
dis	(away from)	appear	_____
ex	(out of)	change	_____
im	(not)	polite	_____
in	(within)	side	_____
mis	(wrong)	place	_____
non	(not)	sense	_____
pre	(before)	school	_____
re	(again)	build	_____
un	(not)	happy	_____

1. Did you go to _____ before kindergarten?

2. The magician made the rabbit _____ .

3. Put your things where they belong so you don't
_____ them.

4. Can you ride a _____ ?

5. Do you want to _____ your shirt for one that fits?

Prefixes and Suffixes

See how many new words you can make by adding prefixes and suffixes to the root words. You can use the prefixes, suffixes and root words as many times as you like.

Prefixes:

bi   dis   ex   in   im   mis   non   pre   re   un

Root Words:

| play | obey | friend | feel | health |
| polite | kind | thought | cycle | like |

Suffixes:

ly   ing   ed   y   ful   ness   less   able   ment

_____   _____

_____   _____

_____   _____

_____   _____

_____   _____

_____   _____

_____   _____

_____   _____

Synonyms

Synonyms are words that mean nearly the same thing. **Start** and **begin** are synonyms.

Find the two words that describe each picture. **Write** the words in the boxes below the picture.

| small | funny | large | sad | silly | little | big | unhappy |

_____   _____

_____   _____

_____   _____

_____   _____

Synonyms

Look at the underlined word in each sentence. **Circle** the word that means nearly the same thing.

1. The <u>little</u> dog ran.   tall   funny   small

2. The <u>happy</u> girl smiled.   glad   sad   good

3. The bird is in the <u>big</u> tree.   green   pretty   tall

4. He was <u>nice</u> to me.   kind   mad   bad

5. The baby is <u>tired</u>.   sleepy   sad   little

Synonyms

Read the sentence that tells about the picture. **Circle** the word that means nearly the same as the word in **bold** letters.

The baby is **unhappy**.

sad   hungry

The flowers are **lovely**.

pretty   green

The child was very **tired**.

sleepy   hurt

The **funny** clown made us laugh.

silly   glad

The ladybug is so **tiny**.

small   red

We saw a **scary** tiger.

frightening   ugly

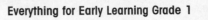

Antonyms

Antonyms are words that are opposites. **Hot** and **cold** are antonyms.

Draw a line between the words that are opposites. Can you think of other words that are opposites?

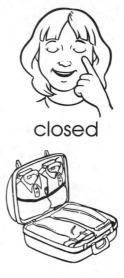

closed

below

full

empty

above

old

new

open

Antonyms

Read the word next to the pictures. **Draw** a line to the word that means the opposite.

dark   empty

hairy   dry

closed   happy

dirty   bald

sad   clean

full   light

wet   open

Antonyms

Dapper Dog is going on a trip. **Write** the antonym for each clue in the crossword puzzle to find where he is going.

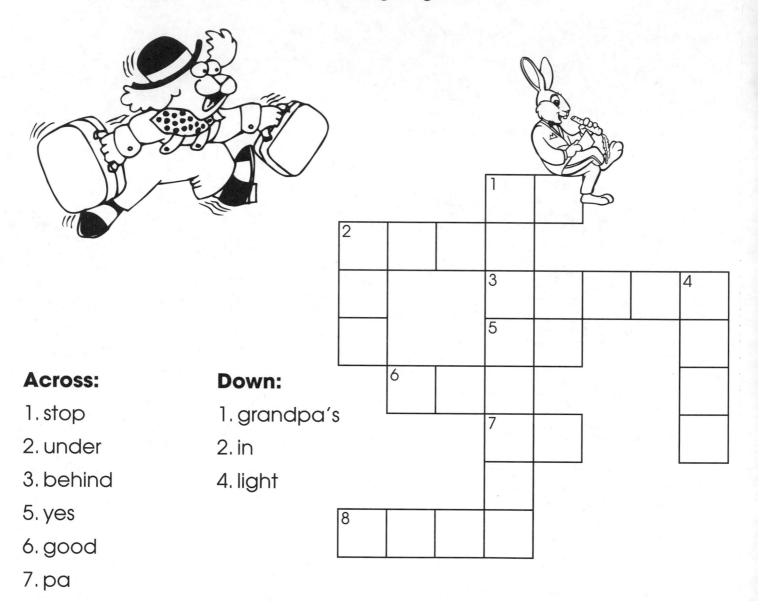

Across:

1. stop
2. under
3. behind
5. yes
6. good
7. pa
8. hit

Down:

1. grandpa's
2. in
4. light

Dapper's answer is hidden in 1 Down. Where is he going?

Homonyms

Homonyms are words that sound the same, but are spelled differently and have different meanings. For example, **sun** and **son** are homonyms.

Look at the word. **Circle** the picture that goes with the word.

1. sun

2. hi

3. ate

4. four

5. buy

6. hear

Homonyms

Look at each picture. **Circle** the homonym that is spelled the correct way.

deer   dear

blue   blew

to   two

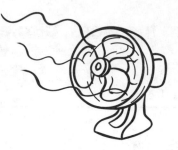

hi   high

by   bye

new   knew

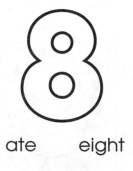

ate   eight

red   read

Homonyms

Write the word from the box that has the same sound but a different meaning next to each picture.

| ball | see | blew | pear |

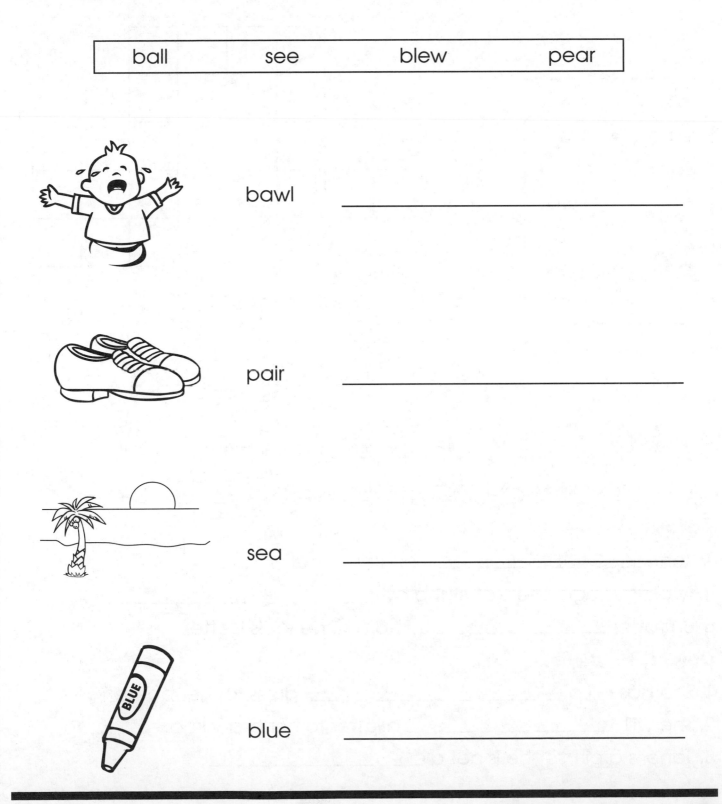

bawl _____

pair _____

sea _____

blue _____

Homonyms

Jane is having a birthday party. Complete each sentence with a homonym from the box. Then, **write** the word in the puzzle.

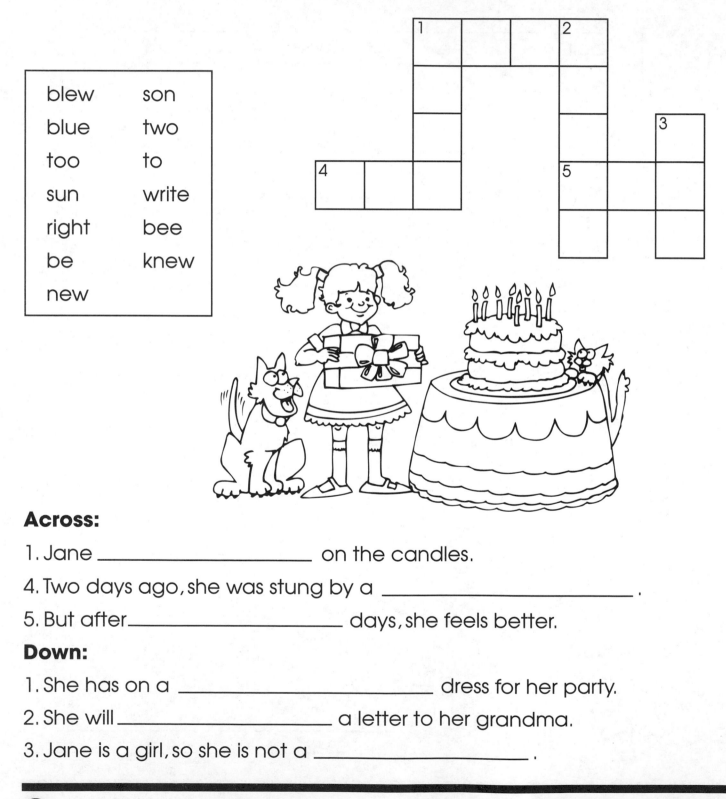

blew	son
blue	two
too	to
sun	write
right	bee
be	knew
new	

Across:

1. Jane _____ on the candles.

4. Two days ago, she was stung by a _____ .

5. But after _____ days, she feels better.

Down:

1. She has on a _____ dress for her party.

2. She will _____ a letter to her grandma.

3. Jane is a girl, so she is not a _____ .

Compound Words

Compound words are two words that are put together to make one new word.

Look at the pictures and read the words that are next to each other. Put the words together to make a new word. **Write** the compound word.

Example:

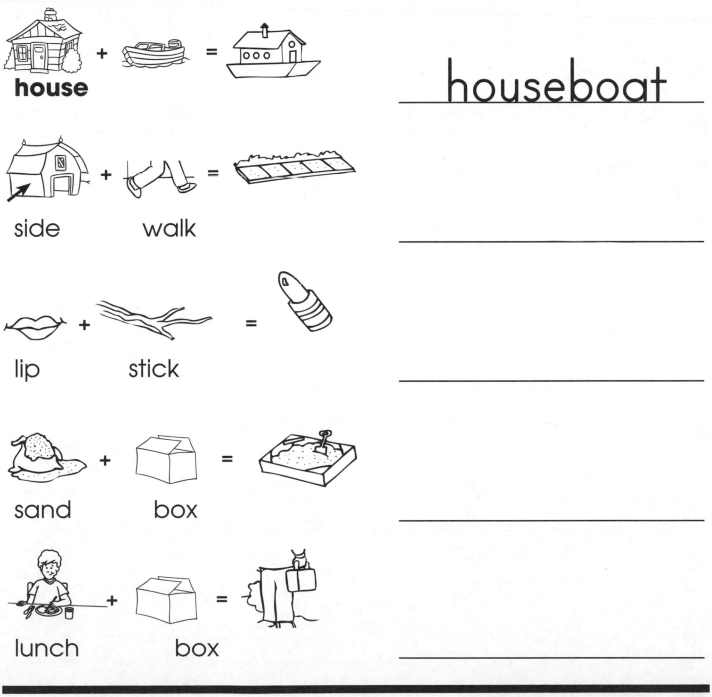

house

houseboat

side   walk

_____

lip   stick

_____

sand   box

_____

lunch   box

_____

Compound Words

Draw lines to make compound words. **Write** the new words on the lines.

Example: song + bird = songbird.

dog   room

foot   box

bed   house

mail   light

some   ball

moon   thing

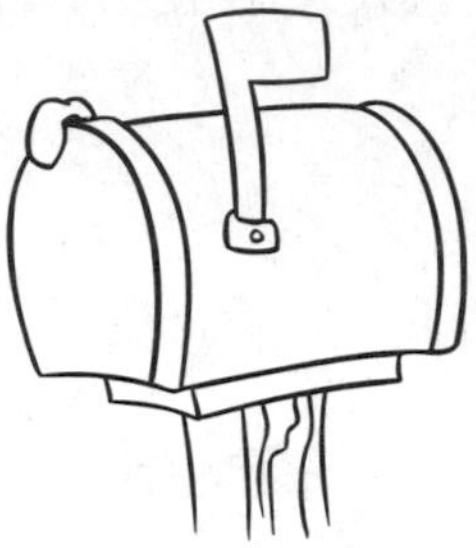

_____   _____

_____   _____

_____   _____

Compound Words

Read the sentences. **Fill in** the blank with a compound word from the word box.

| raincoat | bedroom | lunchbox | hallway | sandbox |

1. A box with sand is a

_____ .

2. The way through a hall is a

_____ .

3. A box for lunch is a

_____ .

4. A coat for the rain is a

_____ .

5. A room with a bed is a

_____ .

Contractions

Contractions are a short way to write two words together. For example, the contraction for the words **it is** is **it's**.

Draw a line from the words to their matching contractions.

I am   she's

it is   they're

you are   we're

we are   he's

they are   I'm

she is   it's

he is   you're

Contractions

We use many contractions with the word **not**.

Example: do not = don't

Draw a line from each word pair to its matching contraction.

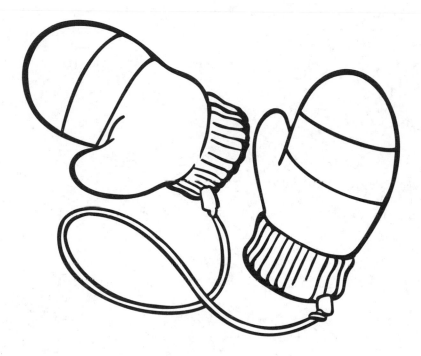

cannot   aren't

do not   can't

will not   don't

are not   won't

Contractions

Help the mother elephants find their babies. **Draw** a line to match the contractions with the words they stand for.

cannot   don't

is not   can't

will not   aren't

are not   won't

I am   couldn't

could not   isn't

do not   I'm

Contractions

Match the words with their contractions.

would not   I've

was not   he'll

he will   wouldn't

could not   wasn't

I have   couldn't

Change the words at the end of each line into contractions to complete the sentences.

1. He _____ know the answer.   **did not**

2. _____ a long way home.   **It is**

3. _____ my house.   **Here is**

4. _____ not going to school today.   **We are**

5. _____ take the bus home tomorrow.   **They will**

DICTIONARY
SKILLS

ABC Order

Sometimes words are put in **ABC order**. That means that if a word starts with **a**, it comes first. If it starts with **b**, it comes next and so on in the order of the alphabet.

Circle the first letter of each word below. Then, **put** the words in ABC order.

ⓒar   ⓑird   moon   two   nest   fan

___bird___   _____   _____

___car___   _____   _____

card   dog   pig   bike   sun   pie

_____   _____   _____

_____   _____   _____

ABC Order

Look at each row of pictures. **Circle** the picture in that row that **comes first** in ABC order. **Underline** the picture that **comes last** in each line.

hat

fish

mittens

pig

duck

wagon

lion

cat

key

glove

pear

snake

tree

grass

bug

leaf

ABC Order

Put each row of words in ABC order. If the first letters of two words are the same, look at the second or third letters.

Example:

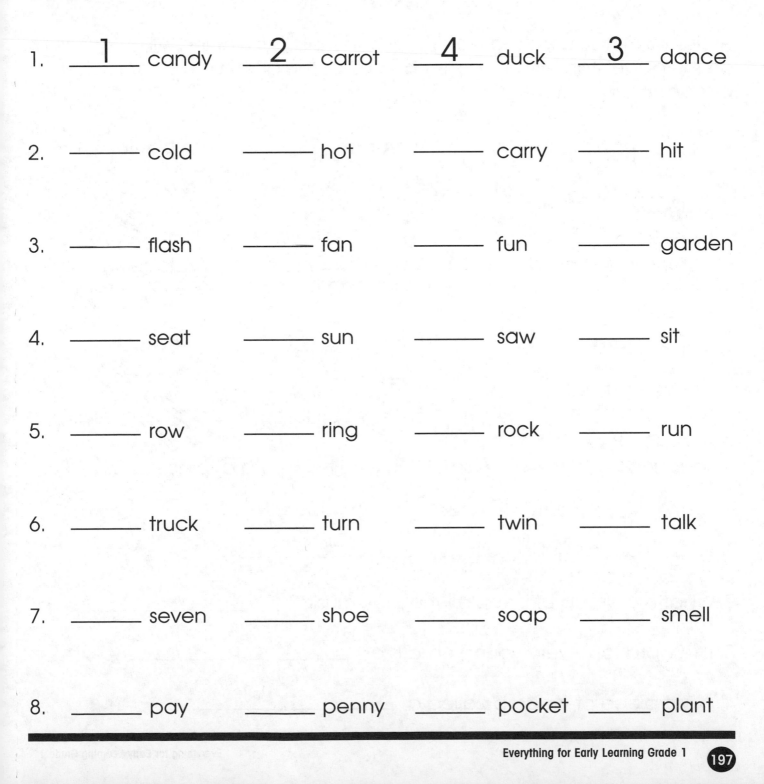

1. __1__ candy   __2__ carrot   __4__ duck   __3__ dance

2. ____ cold   ____ hot   ____ carry   ____ hit

3. ____ flash   ____ fan   ____ fun   ____ garden

4. ____ seat   ____ sun   ____ saw   ____ sit

5. ____ row   ____ ring   ____ rock   ____ run

6. ____ truck   ____ turn   ____ twin   ____ talk

7. ____ seven   ____ shoe   ____ soap   ____ smell

8. ____ pay   ____ penny   ____ pocket   ____ plant

Dictionary Skills

A **dictionary** tells you many things. It tells you what words mean. It also tells you how words are pronounced.

Words in a dictionary are in ABC order. That makes the words easier to find.

A picture dictionary lists a word, its picture and its meaning. All of the words on this page start with the letter **b**. Look at this picture dictionary. Then, **answer** the questions.

baby

A very young child.

band

A group of people who play music.

bank

A place where money is kept.

bark

The sound a dog makes.

berry

A small, juicy fruit.

board

A flat piece of wood.

1. What is a small, juicy fruit? _____ .

2. What is a group of people who play music? _____ .

3. The word for a very young child is a _____ .

4. A flat piece of wood is called a _____ .

Dictionary Skills

The guide word on the left tells what the first word on the page is. The guide word on the right tells what the last word on the page is. Look at the **guide words** in **bold** on this page. Then, look at the words that come between the **guide words**. **Answer** the questions.

---

table   **tiger**

---

table

Furniture with legs and a flat top.

tail

A slender part that is on the back of an animal.

teacher

A person who teaches lessons.

telephone

Something that sends and receives sounds.

ticket

A paper slip or card.

tiger

An animal that has stripes.

1. What are the guide words on this page? _____ and _____

2. Who is a person who teaches lessons? _____

3. Name an animal with stripes. _____

4. What is a piece of furniture with legs and a flat top? _____

Dictionary Skills

Look at the two dictionary pages. What are their guide words? **Put** each word from the box in ABC order between each pair of guide words.

face   **flat**

fix	fan	farm
family	finish	fast
first	feel	fence
few	fight	flag

Syllables

One way to help you read a word you don't know is to divide it into parts called **syllables**. Every syllable has a vowel sound. Remember, vowel teams count as only one vowel sound. One way to count syllables is to clap as you say the word.

Example: strawberry — 3 claps — 3 syllables

Say the words and listen for syllables.
Write the number of syllables. The first
one is done for you.

bird	1	rabbit	_____
apple	_____	elephant	_____
balloon	_____	family	_____
basketball	_____	fence	_____
breakfast	_____	ladder	_____
block	_____	open	_____
candy	_____	puddle	_____
popcorn	_____	Saturday	_____
yellow	_____	wind	_____

Two-Syllable Words

When a **double consonant** is used in the middle of a word, the word can usually be divided between the consonants.

Look at the words in the box. **Divide** each word into two syllables. The first one shows you what to do.

butter	kitten	yellow	dinner
ladder	happy	pillow	mitten

but ter

_____   _____

_____   _____

_____   _____

Many words are divided between two consonants that are not alike.

Look at the words in the box. **Divide** each word into two syllables. The first one shows you what to do.

window	doctor	number	mister
winter	pencil	barber	sister

win dow

_____   _____

_____   _____

_____   _____

CLASSIFICATION

Classification

Draw an **X** on the picture that **does not** belong in each group.

fruit

apple   peach   corn   watermelon

wild animals

bear   kitten   gorilla   lion

pets

cat   fish   elephant   dog

flowers

grass   rose   daisy   tulip

Classification

Dapper Dog is going on a camping trip. **Draw** an **X** on the word in each row that **does not** belong.

1.	flashlight	candle	radio	fire
2.	shirt	pants	coat	bat
3.	cow	car	bus	train
4.	beans	hot dog	ball	bread
5.	gloves	hat	book	boots
6.	fork	butter	cup	plate
7.	book	ball	bat	milk
8.	dogs	bees	flies	ants

Classification

The words in each box form a group. Choose the word from the box that describes each group and **write** it on the line.

| clothes | family | colors | flowers |
| fruits | animals | coins | toys | noises |

rose buttercup tulip daisy _____	crash bang ring pop _____	mother father sister brother _____
puzzle wagon blocks doll _____	green purple blue red _____	grapes orange apple plum _____
shirt socks dress coat _____	dime penny nickel quarter _____	dog horse elephant moose _____

Classification

Write each word in the correct row at the bottom of the page.

car   pencil   chalk   radio   boat   fork

plate   friend   airplane   drum   spoon   crayon

Things we ride in:

_____   _____   _____

Things we eat with:

_____   _____   _____

Things we draw with:

_____   _____   _____

Things we listen to:

_____   _____   _____

Classification

Read the words in the boxes. **Write** each word in its correct place.

Joe	cat	blue	Tim
two	dog	red	ten
Sue	green	pig	six

Name
Words

_____   _____   _____

Number
Words

_____   _____   _____

Animal
Words

_____   _____   _____

Color
Words

_____   _____   _____

NUMBERS AND COUNTING

Sequencing Numbers

Sequencing is putting numbers in the correct order.

Write the missing numbers.

Example: 4, __5__, 6

3, _____, 5   7, _____, 9   8, _____, 10

6, _____, 8   _____, 3, 4   _____, 5, 6

5, 6, _____   _____, 6, 7   _____, 3, 4

_____, 9, 10   _____, 7, 8   2, _____, 4

2, 3, _____   1, 2, _____   7, 8, _____

2, _____, 4   _____, 7, 8   4, _____, 6

6, 7, _____   2, 3, _____   1, _____, 3

7, 8, _____   _____, 3, 4   _____, 9, 10

Counting

Write the number that is:

next in order	one less	one greater
22, 23, _____ , _____	_____ , 16	6, _____
674, _____ , _____	_____ , 247	125, _____
227, _____ , _____	_____ , 550	499, _____
199, _____ , _____	_____ , 333	750, _____
399, _____ , _____	_____ , 862	933, _____

Write the missing numbers.

13   14

163   166

821   823

Number Words

Number the buildings from one to six.

Draw a line from the word to the number.

two	1
five	3
six	5
four	6
one	2
three	4

Number Words

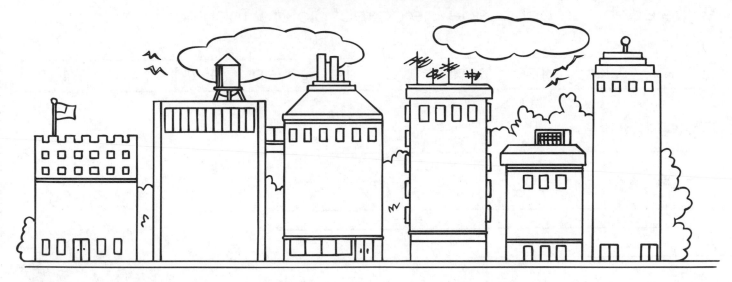

Number the buildings from five to ten.

Draw a line from the word to the number.

nine   8

seven   10

five   7

eight   5

six   9

ten   6

Number Words

Write each number beside the correct picture. Then, **write** it again.

| one | two | three | four | five | six | seven | eight | nine | ten |

Example:

$\overline{\text{six}}$ $\overline{\text{six}}$

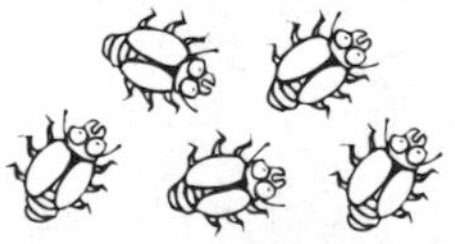

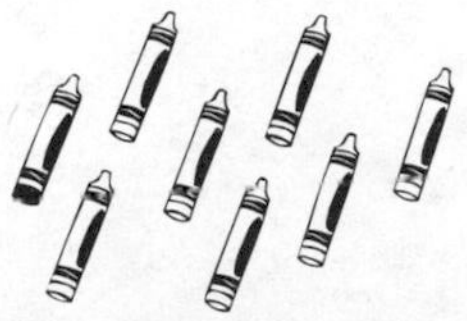

Counting by Fives

Count by fives to **draw** the path to the playground.

Counting by Tens

Count by tens to **draw** the path to the store.

Counting by Twos, Fives and Tens

Write the missing numbers.

Count by 2's:

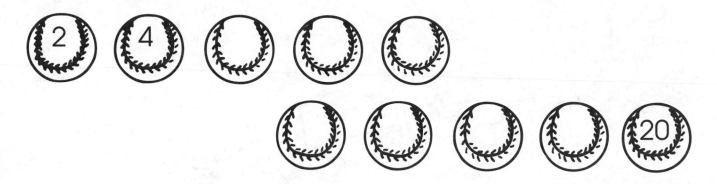

Count by 5's:

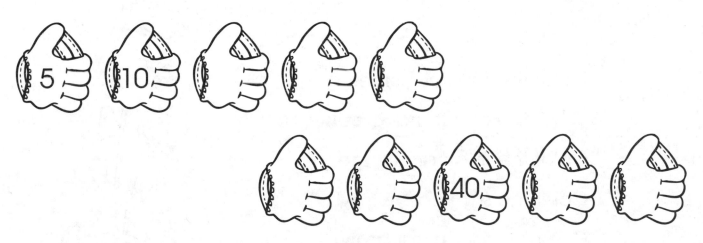

Count by 10's:

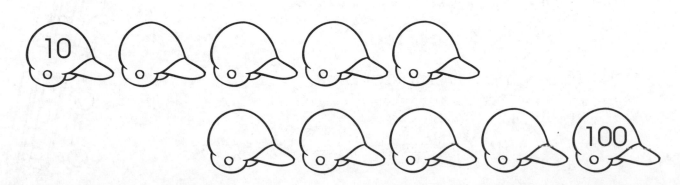

Ordinal Numbers

Ordinal numbers show the order in a series, such as **first**, **second** or **third**. Follow the instructions to **color** the train cars. The first car is the engine.

Color the third car **blue**.

Color the eighth car **green**.

Color the fifth car **orange**.

Color the sixth car **yellow**.

Color the fourth car **brown**.

Color the second car **purple**.

Color the first car **red**.

Color the seventh car **pink**.

Ordinal Numbers

Write each word on the correct line to put the words in order.

second	fifth	seventh	first	tenth
third	eighth	sixth	fourth	ninth

1. _____   6. _____

2. _____   7. _____

3. _____   8. _____

4. _____   9. _____

5. _____   10. _____

Which picture is circled in each row? **Underline** the word that tells the correct number.

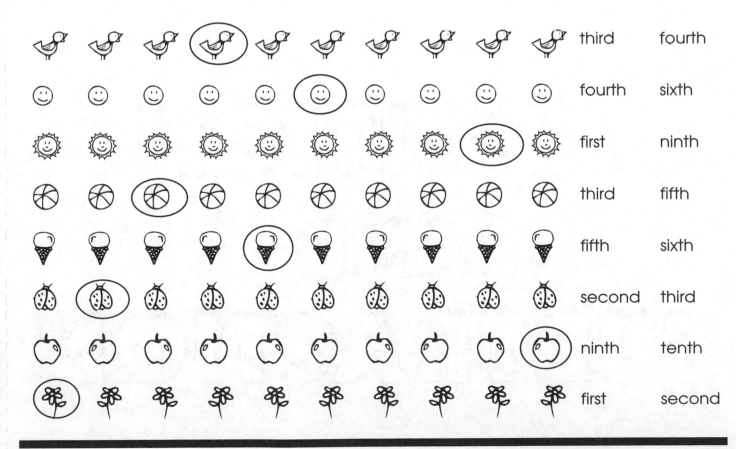

third   fourth

fourth   sixth

first   ninth

third   fifth

fifth   sixth

second   third

ninth   tenth

first   second

ADDITION AND SUBTRACTION

Addition

Addition means **putting together** or adding two or more numbers to find the sum.

Count the cats and **write** how many.

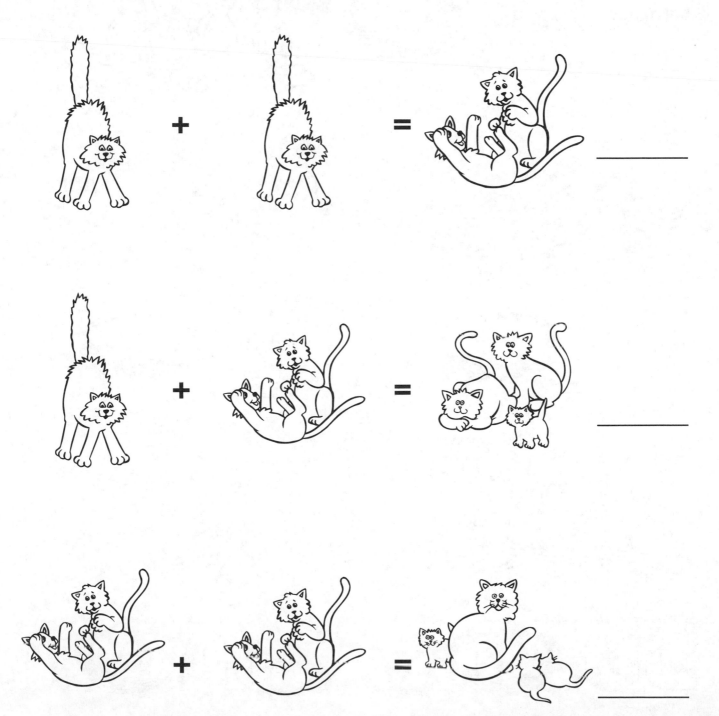

Addition

Add the numbers. Write your answers in the nests.

Example: $2 + 3 =$ 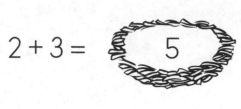 5

$1 + 2 =$

$1 + 3 =$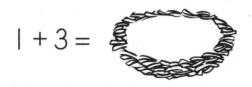

$4 + 1 =$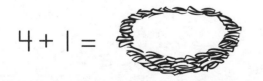

$1 + 1 =$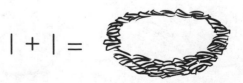

Addition

Practice writing the numbers. Then, **add** the numbers and **write** the sum.

3

4

5

6

$$\begin{array}{r} 2 \\ +4 \\ \hline \end{array}$$

$$\begin{array}{r} 1 \\ +4 \\ \hline \end{array}$$

$$\begin{array}{r} 2 \\ +2 \\ \hline \end{array}$$

$$\begin{array}{r} 1 \\ +2 \\ \hline \end{array}$$

Addition

Practice writing the numbers. Then, **add** the numbers and **write** the sum.

4

5

6

7

$$\begin{array}{r} 2 \\ +5 \\ \hline \end{array}$$

$$\begin{array}{r} 3 \\ +1 \\ \hline \end{array}$$

$$\begin{array}{r} 4 \\ +1 \\ \hline \end{array}$$

$$\begin{array}{r} 2 \\ +4 \\ \hline \end{array}$$

Addition

Practice writing the numbers. Then, **add** the numbers and **write** the sum.

6

7

8

$$3$$
$$+4$$
―――

$$5$$
$$+1$$
―――

$$2$$
$$+6$$
―――

$$4$$
$$+4$$
―――

Addition

Practice writing the numbers. Then, **add** the numbers and **write** the sum.

7 _____

8 _____

8 _____

q _____

$$\begin{array}{r} 8 \\ +1 \\ \hline \end{array}$$

$$\begin{array}{r} 3 \\ +5 \\ \hline \end{array}$$

$$\begin{array}{r} 2 \\ +7 \\ \hline \end{array}$$

$$\begin{array}{r} 6 \\ +1 \\ \hline \end{array}$$

Addition

Add the numbers. **Write** your answers in the doghouses.

Example:

$4 + 2 =$

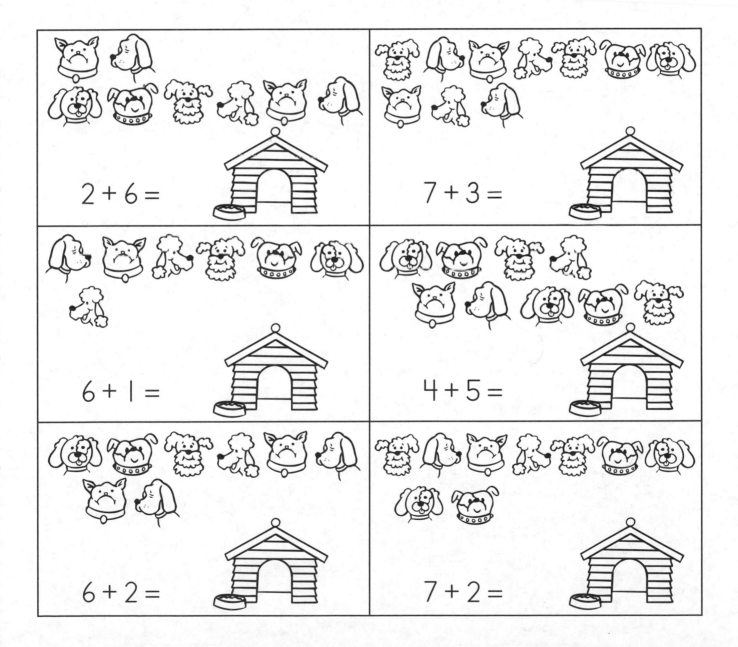

$2 + 6 =$

$7 + 3 =$

$6 + 1 =$

$4 + 5 =$

$6 + 2 =$

$7 + 2 =$

Addition

Solve the number problem under each picture.

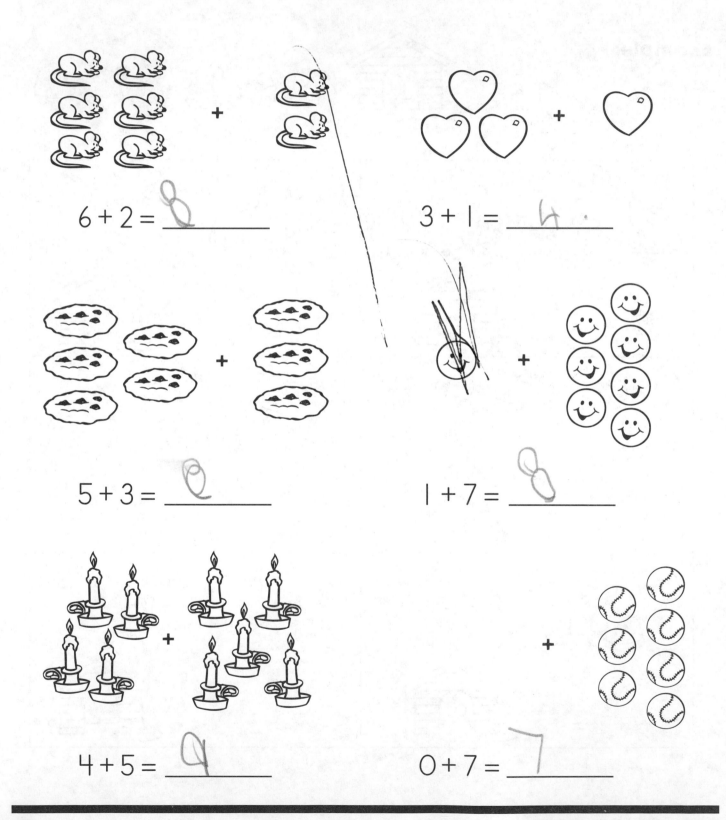

6 + 2 = _____

3 + 1 = _____

5 + 3 = _____

1 + 7 = _____

4 + 5 = _____

0 + 7 = _____

Addition

Solve the number problem under each picture.

$1 + 3 =$ _____

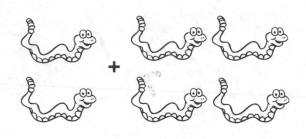

$2 + 4 =$ _____

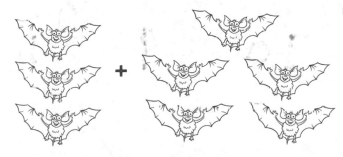

$3 + 5 =$ _____

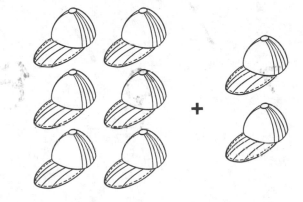

$6 + 2 =$ _____

$8 + 1 =$ _____

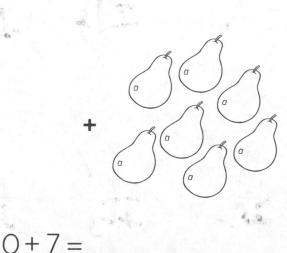

$0 + 7 =$ _____

Addition

Add the numbers. Then, **write** the sum.

Example:

$$\begin{array}{r} 2 \\ +5 \\ \hline 7 \end{array}$$

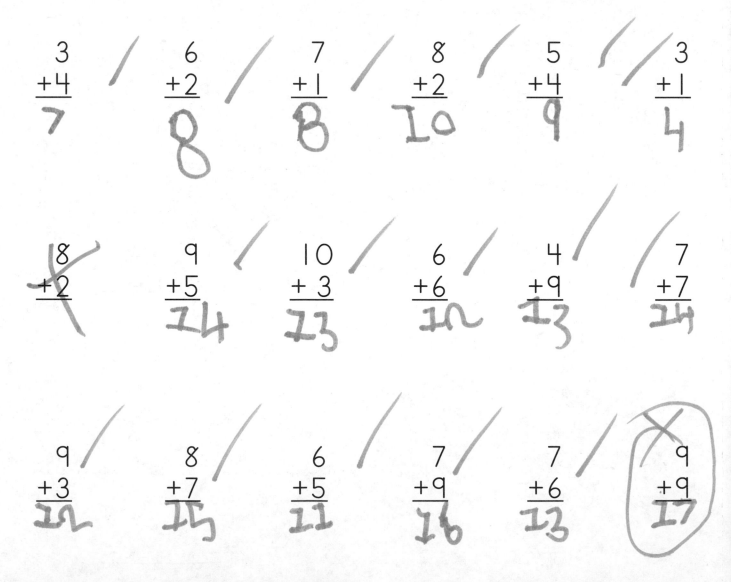

3 $+4$ $\overline{7}$	6 $+2$ $\overline{8}$	7 $+1$ $\overline{8}$	8 $+2$ $\overline{10}$	5 $+4$ $\overline{9}$	3 $+1$ $\overline{4}$
8 $+2$	9 $+5$ $\overline{14}$	10 $+3$ $\overline{13}$	6 $+6$ $\overline{12}$	4 $+9$ $\overline{13}$	7 $+7$ $\overline{14}$
9 $+3$ $\overline{12}$	8 $+7$ $\overline{15}$	6 $+5$ $\overline{11}$	7 $+9$ $\overline{16}$	7 $+6$ $\overline{13}$	9 $+9$ $\overline{17}$

Subtraction

Subtraction means **taking away** or subtracting one number from another to find the difference.

Practice writing the numbers. Then, **subtract** the numbers and **write** the difference.

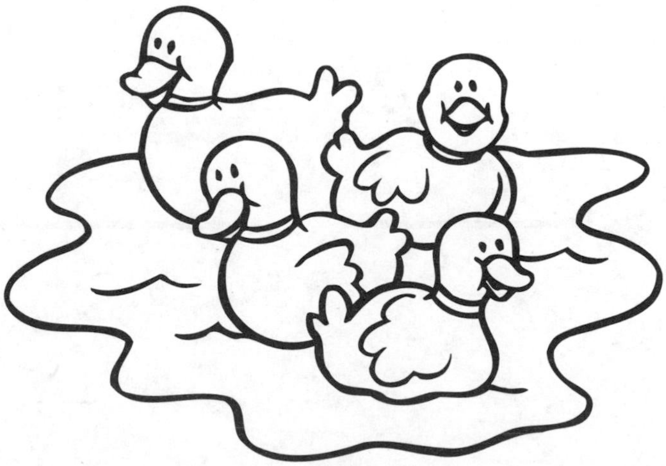

1 ------------------

2 ------------------

3 ------------------

$$3 - 1$$

$$4 - 3$$

$$2 - 1$$

$$5 - 2$$

Subtraction

Practice writing the numbers. Then, **subtract** the numbers and **write** the difference.

3

4

5

6

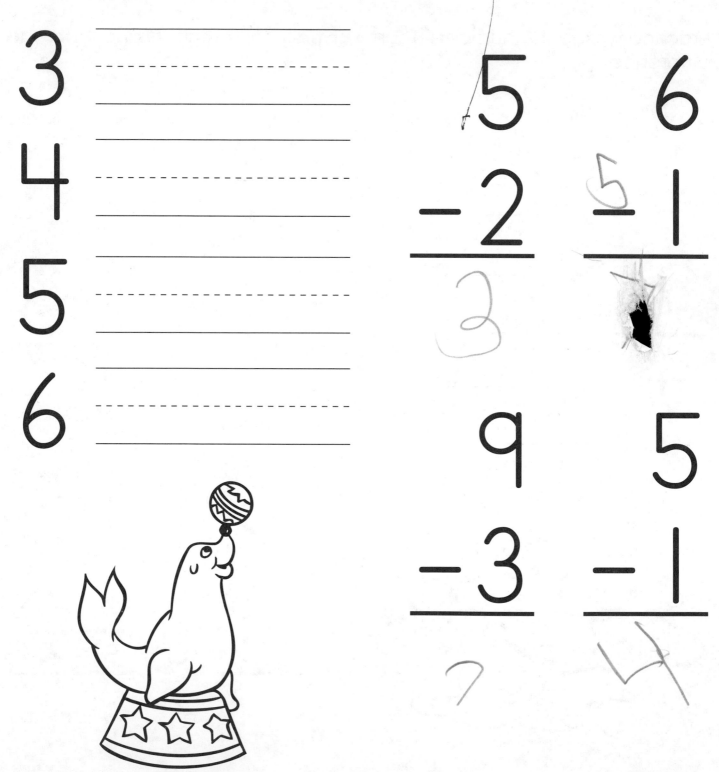

$$5$$
$$-2$$
$$\overline{}$$
3

$$6$$
$$-1$$

$$9$$
$$-3$$
2

$$5$$
$$-1$$
4

Subtraction

Count the flowers. **Write** your answer on the blank. **Circle** the problem with the same answer.

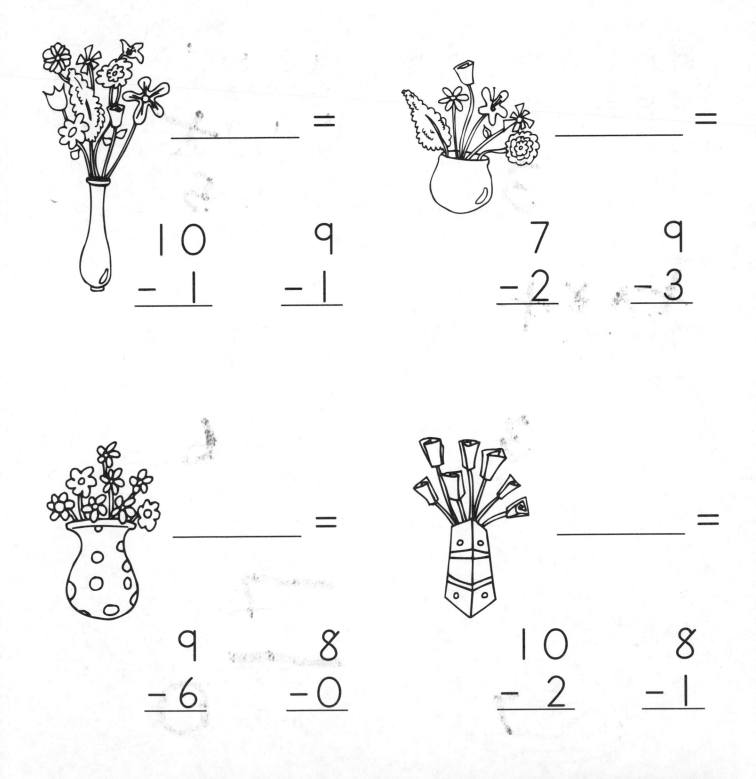

$$\underline{\qquad} =$$

$$\begin{array}{c} 10 \\ -1 \\ \hline \end{array} \qquad \begin{array}{c} 9 \\ -1 \\ \hline \end{array}$$

$$\underline{\qquad} =$$

$$\begin{array}{c} 7 \\ -2 \\ \hline \end{array} \qquad \begin{array}{c} 9 \\ -3 \\ \hline \end{array}$$

$$\underline{\qquad} =$$

$$\begin{array}{c} 9 \\ -6 \\ \hline \end{array} \qquad \begin{array}{c} 8 \\ -0 \\ \hline \end{array}$$

$$\underline{\qquad} =$$

$$\begin{array}{c} 10 \\ -2 \\ \hline \end{array} \qquad \begin{array}{c} 8 \\ -1 \\ \hline \end{array}$$

Subtraction

Solve the number problem under each picture.

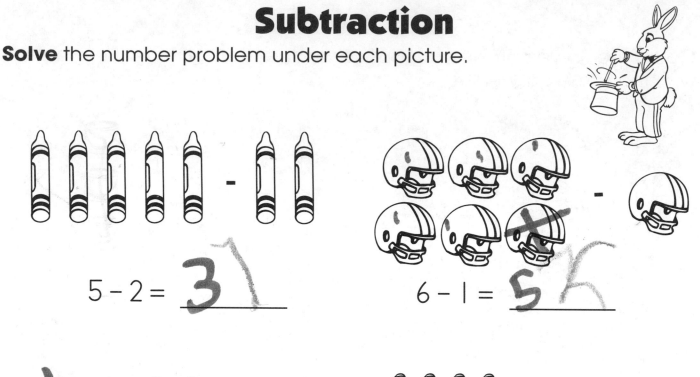

$5 - 2 =$ **3**

$6 - 1 =$ **5**

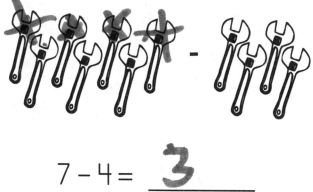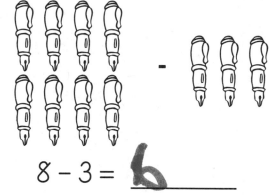

$7 - 4 =$ **3**

$8 - 3 =$ **6**

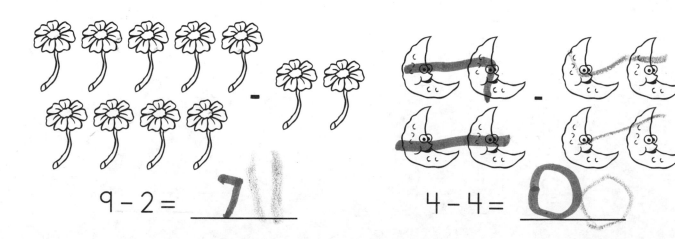

$9 - 2 =$ **7**

$4 - 4 =$ **0**

Subtraction

Solve the number problem under each picture.

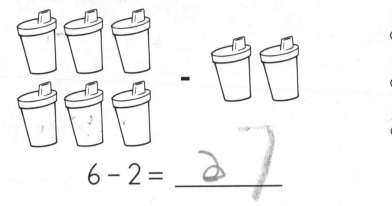

$6 - 2 =$ 2

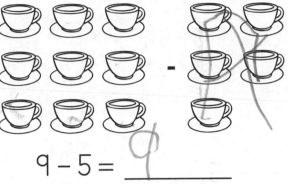

$9 - 5 =$ 9

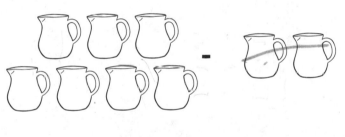

$7 - 2 =$ 7

$4 - 1 =$ 4

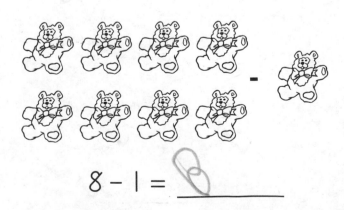

$8 - 1 =$ 8

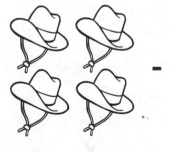

$4 - 0 =$ 4

Good work

Subtraction

Subtract.

Example:

$$\begin{array}{r} 4 \\ -3 \\ \hline \end{array}$$

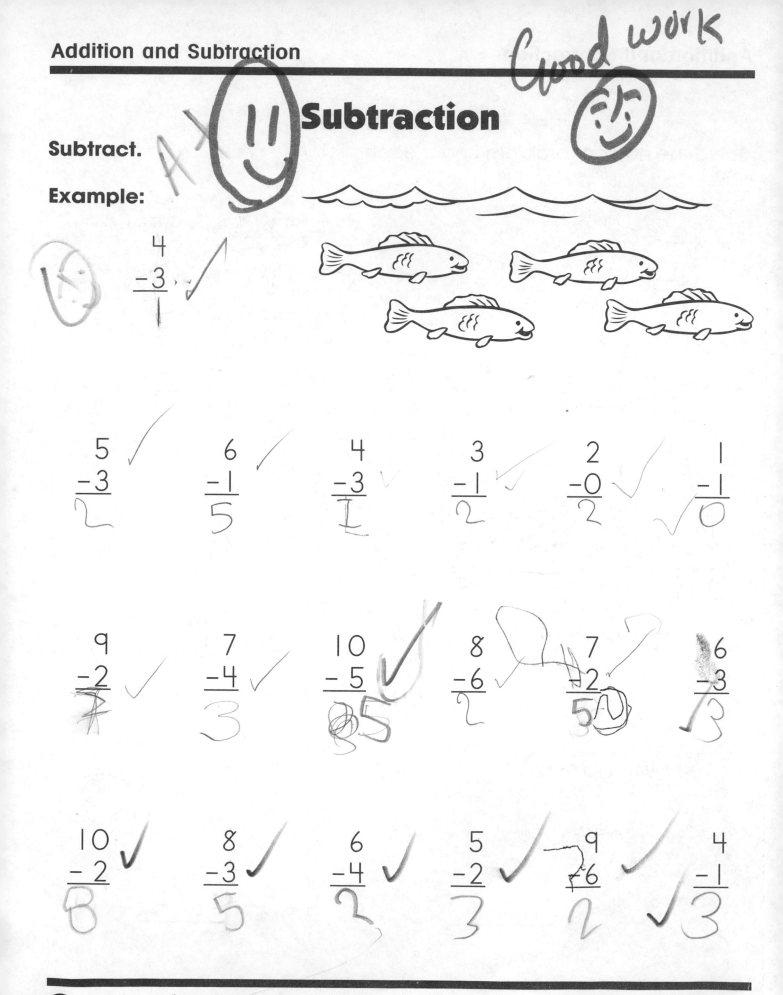

$$\begin{array}{r} 5 \\ -3 \\ \hline 2 \end{array} \quad \begin{array}{r} 6 \\ -1 \\ \hline 5 \end{array} \quad \begin{array}{r} 4 \\ -3 \\ \hline 1 \end{array} \quad \begin{array}{r} 3 \\ -1 \\ \hline 2 \end{array} \quad \begin{array}{r} 2 \\ -0 \\ \hline 2 \end{array} \quad \begin{array}{r} 1 \\ -1 \\ \hline 0 \end{array}$$

$$\begin{array}{r} 9 \\ -2 \\ \hline 7 \end{array} \quad \begin{array}{r} 7 \\ -4 \\ \hline 3 \end{array} \quad \begin{array}{r} 10 \\ -5 \\ \hline 5 \end{array} \quad \begin{array}{r} 8 \\ -6 \\ \hline 2 \end{array} \quad \begin{array}{r} 7 \\ -2 \\ \hline 5 \end{array} \quad \begin{array}{r} 6 \\ -3 \\ \hline 3 \end{array}$$

$$\begin{array}{r} 10 \\ -2 \\ \hline 8 \end{array} \quad \begin{array}{r} 8 \\ -3 \\ \hline 5 \end{array} \quad \begin{array}{r} 6 \\ -4 \\ \hline 2 \end{array} \quad \begin{array}{r} 5 \\ -2 \\ \hline 3 \end{array} \quad \begin{array}{r} 9 \\ -6 \\ \hline 2 \end{array} \quad \begin{array}{r} 4 \\ -1 \\ \hline 3 \end{array}$$

Addition and Subtraction

Solve the number problem under each picture.

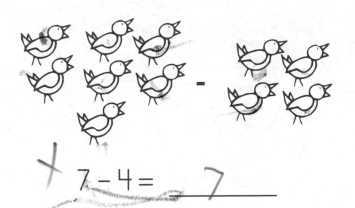

$$7 - 4 = \quad 7$$

$$1 + 4 = \quad 5 \checkmark$$

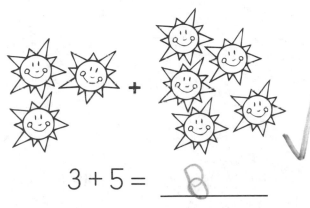

$$3 + 5 = \quad 8 \checkmark$$

$$8 - 1 = \quad 9$$

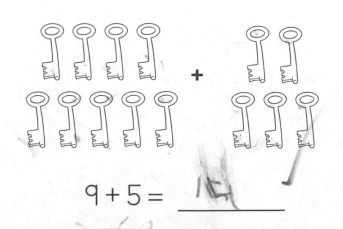

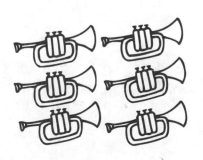

$$9 + 5 = \quad 14$$

$$6 - 3 = \quad 6$$

Addition and Subtraction

Solve the number problem under each picture. **Write +** or **-** to show if you should add or subtract.

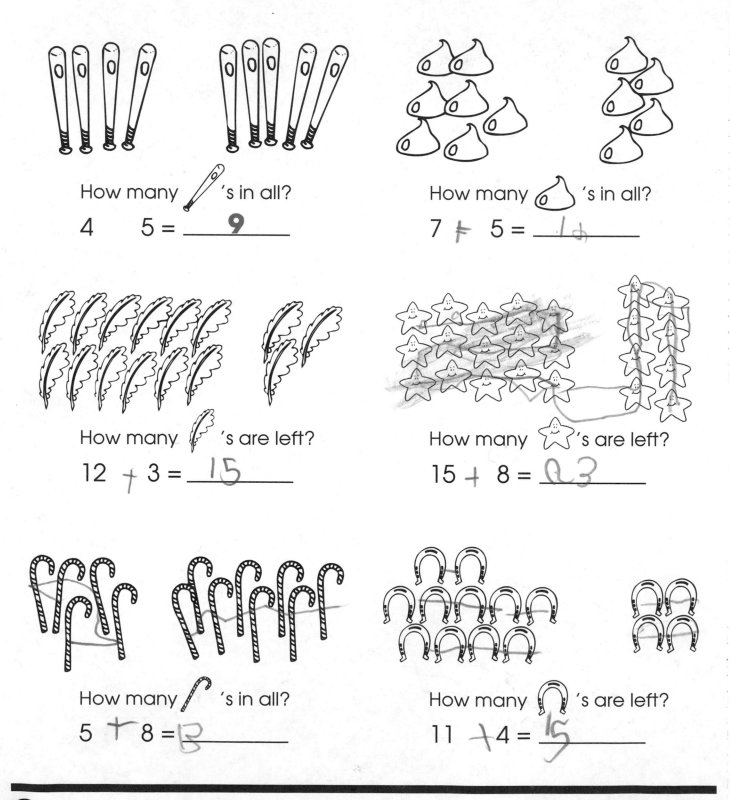

How many ⚾'s in all?

4   5 = ___9___

How many 🍫's in all?

7 + 5 = ___12___

How many 🌿's are left?

12 + 3 = ___15___

How many ⭐'s are left?

15 + 8 = ___23___

How many 🍬's in all?

5 + 8 = ___13___

How many 🧲's are left?

11 + 4 = ___15___

Addition and Subtraction

Solve the number problem under each picture. **Write +** or **-** to show if you should add or subtract.

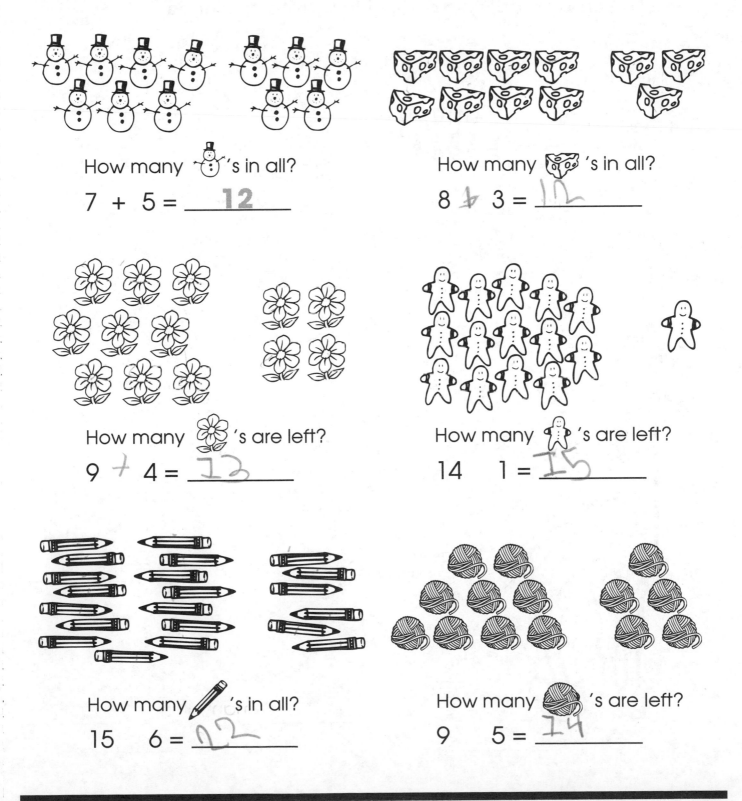

How many 's in all?

7 + 5 = __12__

How many 's in all?

8 + 3 = __12__

How many 's are left?

9 + 4 = __13__

How many 's are left?

14   1 = __15__

How many 's in all?

15   6 = __22__

How many 's are left?

9   5 = __14__

Addition and Subtraction

Solve the problems. **Remember**, addition means putting together or adding two or more numbers to find the sum. Subtraction means taking away or subtracting one number from another to find the difference.

$1 + 3 =$ _____ $4 - 3 =$ _____ $4 + 5 =$ _____

$6 + 1 =$ _____ $7 - 2 =$ _____ $8 - 4 =$ _____

$9 - 1 =$ _____ $10 - 3 =$ _____

$5 - 2 =$ _____ $6 + 3 =$ _____

$8 + 2 =$ _____ $5 + 5 =$ _____

Addition and Subtraction

Add or subtract. **Circle** the answers that are less than 10.

Examples:

$$\begin{array}{r} 3 \\ +1 \\ \hline 4 \end{array}$$

$$\begin{array}{r} 3 \\ -1 \\ \hline 2 \end{array}$$

$$\begin{array}{r} 9 \\ +3 \\ \hline \end{array} \qquad \begin{array}{r} 6 \\ -2 \\ \hline \end{array} \qquad \begin{array}{r} 12 \\ -1 \\ \hline \end{array} \qquad \begin{array}{r} 18 \\ +1 \\ \hline \end{array} \qquad \begin{array}{r} 15 \\ -6 \\ \hline \end{array}$$

$$\begin{array}{r} 7 \\ +6 \\ \hline \end{array} \qquad \begin{array}{r} 16 \\ -9 \\ \hline \end{array} \qquad \begin{array}{r} 10 \\ -3 \\ \hline \end{array} \qquad \begin{array}{r} 14 \\ +5 \\ \hline \end{array} \qquad \begin{array}{r} 16 \\ -8 \\ \hline \end{array}$$

$$\begin{array}{r} 8 \\ +7 \\ \hline \end{array} \qquad \begin{array}{r} 12 \\ +2 \\ \hline \end{array} \qquad \begin{array}{r} 13 \\ -4 \\ \hline \end{array} \qquad \begin{array}{r} 17 \\ +2 \\ \hline \end{array} \qquad \begin{array}{r} 9 \\ +9 \\ \hline \end{array}$$

Addition and Subtraction

Solve the problems. Use the code to color the quilt.

Color: 6 = blue   7 = yellow   8 = green   9 = red   10 = orange

PLACE VALUE

Tens and Ones

The **place value** of a number is shown by where it is in the number. For example, in the number **23**, **2** has the place value of **tens** and **3** is the number of **ones**.

Count the groups of ten crayons and **write** the number by the word **tens**. Count the other crayons and **write** the number by the word **ones**.

Example:

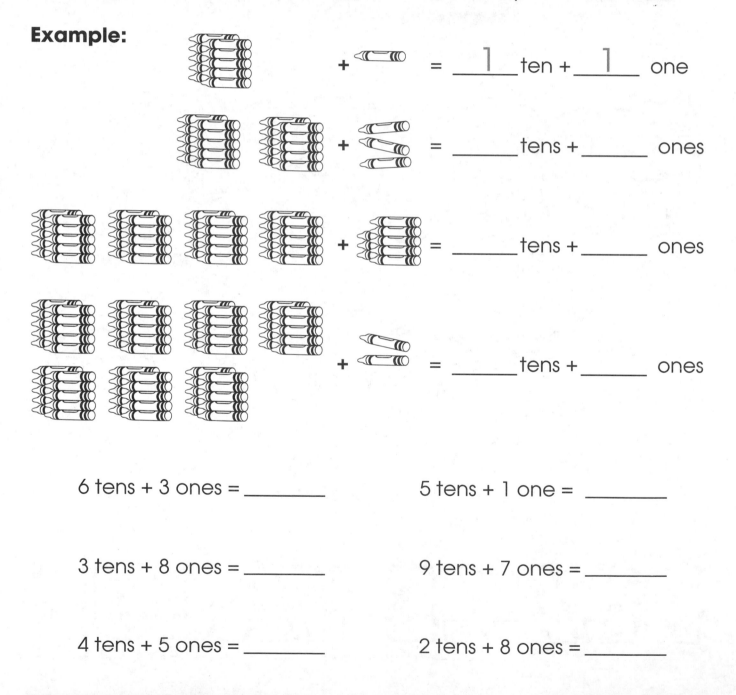

= _____1_____ ten + _____1_____ one

= _____ tens + _____ ones

= _____ tens + _____ ones

= _____ tens + _____ ones

6 tens + 3 ones = _____   5 tens + 1 one = _____

3 tens + 8 ones = _____   9 tens + 7 ones = _____

4 tens + 5 ones = _____   2 tens + 8 ones = _____

Tens and Ones

Write the answers in the correct spaces.

	tens	ones	

3 tens, 2 ones   _____   _____   = _____

3 tens, 7 ones   _____   _____   = _____

9 tens, 1 one   _____   _____   = _____

5 tens, 6 ones   _____   _____   = _____

6 tens, 5 ones   _____   _____   = _____

6 tens, 8 ones   _____   _____   = _____

2 tens, 8 ones   _____   _____   = _____

4 tens, 9 ones   _____   _____   = _____

1 ten, 4 ones   _____   _____   = _____

8 tens, 2 ones   _____   _____   = _____

4 tens, 2 ones   _____   _____   = _____

28 = _____ tens, _____ ones   38 = _____ tens, _____ ones

64 = _____ tens, _____ ones   17 = _____ tens, _____ ones

56 = _____ tens, _____ ones   63 = _____ tens, _____ ones

72 = _____ tens, _____ ones   12 = _____ tens, _____ ones

Tens and Ones

Combine the ones and tens. **Write** your answer on the blank.

Example:

3 tens   +   3 ones   =   33

+   =   33

7 tens + 5 ones = _____   4 tens + 0 ones = _____

2 tens + 3 ones = _____   8 tens + 1 one = _____

5 tens + 2 ones = _____   1 ten + 1 one = _____

5 tens + 4 ones = _____   6 tens + 3 ones = _____

9 tens + 5 ones = _____   3 tens + 7 ones = _____

Draw a line to the correct number.

6 tens + 7 ones   73

4 tens + 2 ones   67

8 tens + 0 ones   51

7 tens + 3 ones   80

5 tens + 1 one   42

Hundreds, Tens and Ones

Count the groups of crayons and **add**.

Example:

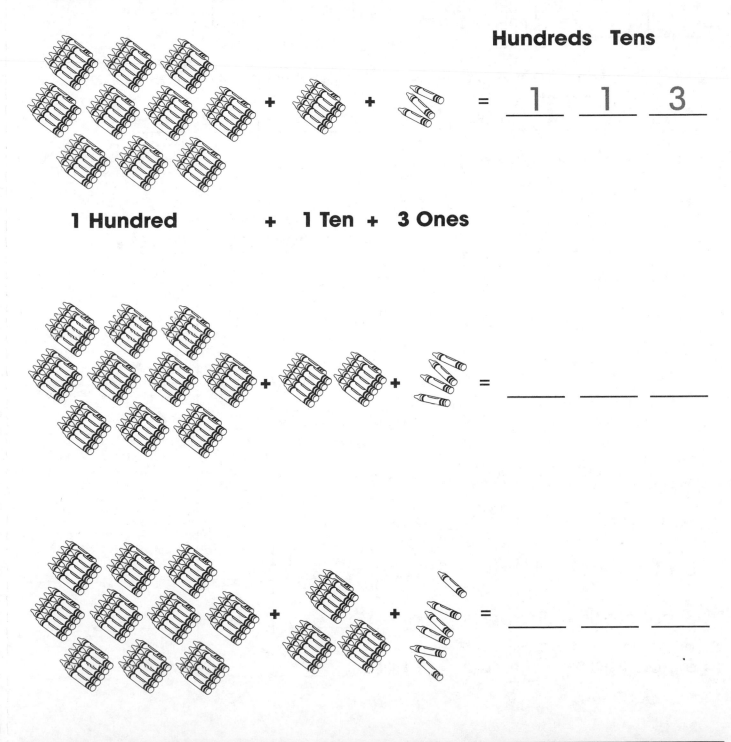

Hundreds   Tens

+ + = __1__ __1__ __3__

1 Hundred + **1 Ten** + **3 Ones**

Hundreds, Tens and Ones

Look at the examples. Then, **write** the missing numbers in the blanks.

Examples:

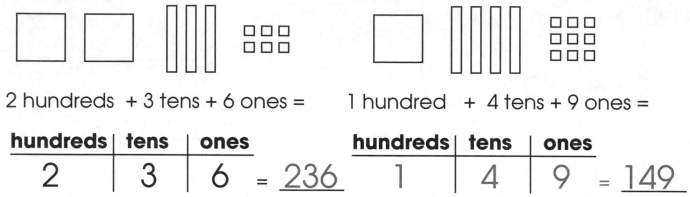

2 hundreds + 3 tens + 6 ones =   1 hundred + 4 tens + 9 ones =

hundreds	tens	ones		hundreds	tens	ones
2	3	6	= 236	1	4	9	= 149

	hundreds	tens	ones	
3 hundreds + 4 tens + 8 ones =	3	4	8	= _____
___ hundreds + ___ ten + ___ ones =	2	1	7	= _____
___ hundreds + ___ tens + ___ ones =	6	3	5	= _____
___ hundreds + ___ tens + ___ ones =	4	7	9	= _____
___ hundreds + ___ tens + ___ ones =	2	9	4	= _____
___ hundreds + ___ tens + ___ ones =	4	___	___	= _____
3 hundreds + 1 ten + 3 ones = ____	____	____	= _____
3 hundreds + ___ tens + 7 ones = ____	5	____	= _____
6 hundreds + 2 tens + ___ ones = ____	____	8	= _____

Thousands, Hundreds, Tens and Ones

Look at the examples. Then, **write** the missing numbers in the blanks.

Example:

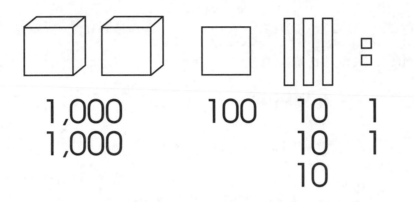

1,000   100   10   1
1,000   10   1
                    10

2 thousands + 1 hundred + __3__ tens + 2 ones = __2,132__

5,286 = _____ thousands + _____ hundreds + _____ tens + _____ one

1,831 = _____ thousand + _____ hundreds + _____ tens + _____ one

8,972 = _____ thousands + _____ hundreds + _____ tens + _____ ones

4,528 = _____ thousands + _____ hundreds + _____ tens + _____ ones

3,177 = _____ thousands + _____ hundred + _____ tens + _____ ones

Draw a line to the number that has:

        8 hundreds   7,103

        5 ones   2,862

        9 tens   5,996

        7 thousands   1,485

Thousands, Hundreds, Tens and Ones

Use the code to **color** the fan.

If the answer has:

9 thousands, color it **pink**.

6 thousands, color it **green**.

5 hundreds, color it **orange**.

8 tens, color it **red**.

3 ones, color it **blue**.

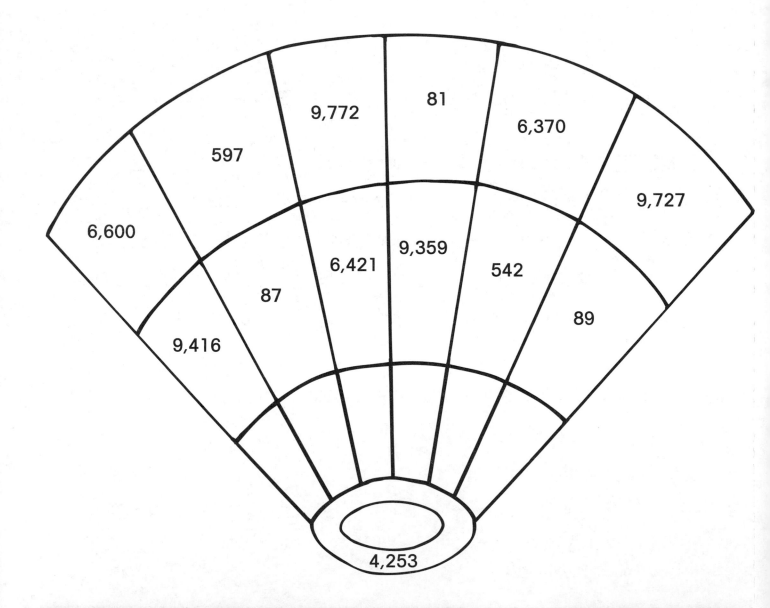

Two-Digit Addition

Look at the example. Follow the steps to add.

Examples:
$$\begin{array}{r} 33 \\ +41 \\ \hline \end{array}$$

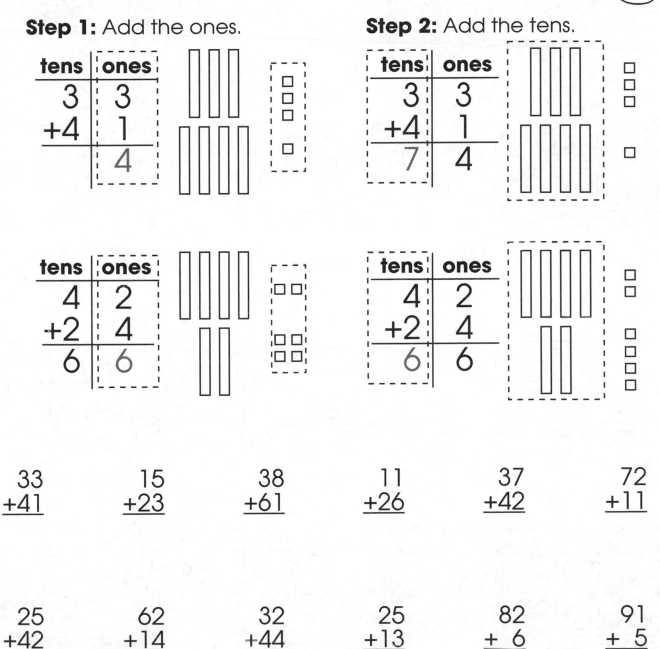

Step 1: Add the ones.

tens	ones
3	3
+4	1
	4

Step 2: Add the tens.

tens	ones
3	3
+4	1
7	4

tens	ones
4	2
+2	4
6	6

tens	ones
4	2
+2	4
6	6

$$\begin{array}{r} 33 \\ +41 \\ \hline \end{array} \qquad \begin{array}{r} 15 \\ +23 \\ \hline \end{array} \qquad \begin{array}{r} 38 \\ +61 \\ \hline \end{array} \qquad \begin{array}{r} 11 \\ +26 \\ \hline \end{array} \qquad \begin{array}{r} 37 \\ +42 \\ \hline \end{array} \qquad \begin{array}{r} 72 \\ +11 \\ \hline \end{array}$$

$$\begin{array}{r} 25 \\ +42 \\ \hline \end{array} \qquad \begin{array}{r} 62 \\ +14 \\ \hline \end{array} \qquad \begin{array}{r} 32 \\ +44 \\ \hline \end{array} \qquad \begin{array}{r} 25 \\ +13 \\ \hline \end{array} \qquad \begin{array}{r} 82 \\ + 6 \\ \hline \end{array} \qquad \begin{array}{r} 91 \\ + 5 \\ \hline \end{array}$$

Two-Digit Addition

Add the total points scored in each game. Remember to add **ones** first and **tens** second.

Example:

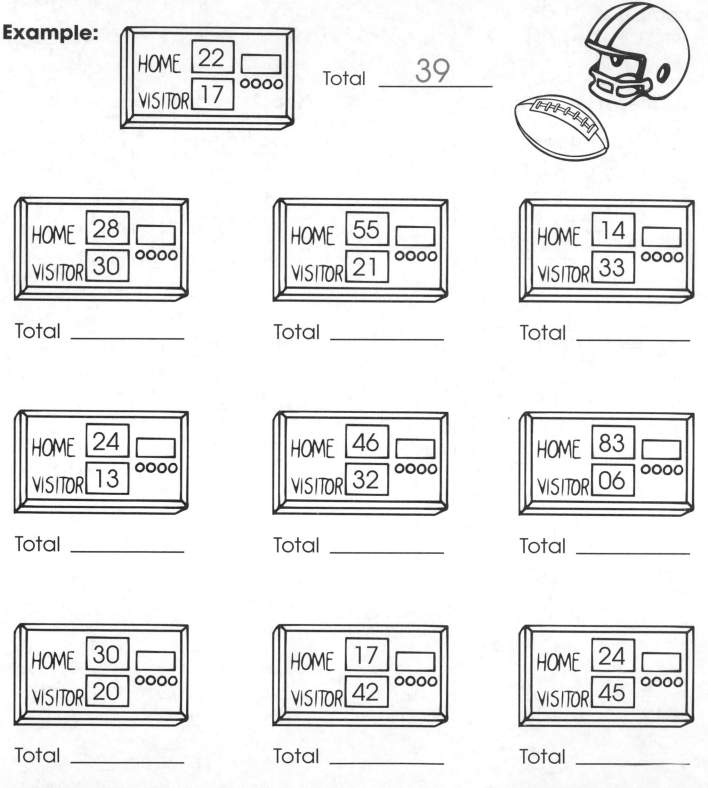

HOME 22
VISITOR 17
Total ___39___

HOME 28
VISITOR 30
Total _____

HOME 55
VISITOR 21
Total _____

HOME 14
VISITOR 33
Total _____

HOME 24
VISITOR 13
Total _____

HOME 46
VISITOR 32
Total _____

HOME 83
VISITOR 06
Total _____

HOME 30
VISITOR 20
Total _____

HOME 17
VISITOR 42
Total _____

HOME 24
VISITOR 45
Total _____

Two-Digit Addition

Addition is putting together or adding two or more numbers to find the sum. **Regrouping** is using **ten ones** to form **one 10**, **ten tens** to form **one hundred** and so on.

Look at the examples. Follow the steps to add.

Examples: 14
             + 8

Step 1: Add the ones.   **Step 2:** Regroup the tens.   **Step 3:** Add the tens.

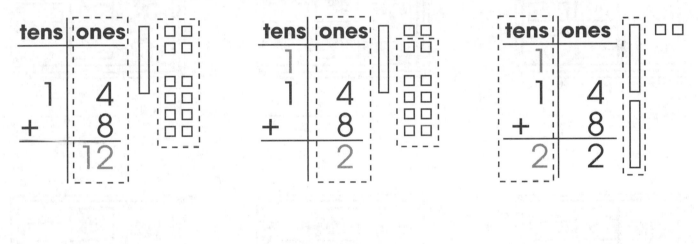

	tens	ones
	1	6
+3		7
		13

	tens	ones
	1	
	1	6
+3		7
		3

	tens	ones
	1	
	1	6
+3		7
	5	3

28	32	54	19	44	25
+17	+38	+25	+55	+ 48	+ 64

Two-Digit Addition

Add the total points scored in the game. Remember to add the **ones** first, and then regroup. Then, add the **tens**.

Example:

HOME 47
VISITOR 38

Total ___85___

HOME 33
VISITOR 57

Total _____

HOME 43
VISITOR 49

Total _____

HOME 57
VISITOR 34

Total _____

HOME 29
VISITOR 22

Total _____

HOME 36
VISITOR 58

Total _____

HOME 45
VISITOR 39

Total _____

HOME 66
VISITOR 26

Total _____

HOME 72
VISITOR 19

Total _____

HOME 54
VISITOR 26

Total _____

Two-Digit Subtraction

Look at the example. Follow the steps to subtract.

Examples:
$$\begin{array}{r} 28 \\ -14 \\ \hline \end{array}$$

Step 1: Subtract the ones.

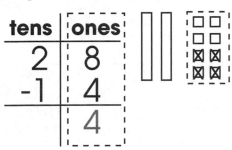

Step 2: Subtract the tens.

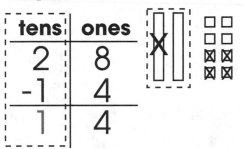

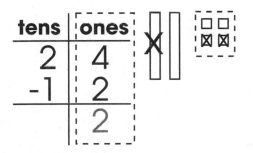

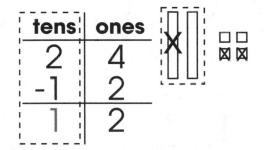

24	61	77	85	57	87
-12	-30	-44	-24	-23	-33

29	74	46	69	95	33
-15	-51	-32	-35	-32	-33

Two-Digit Subtraction

Subtraction is taking away or subtracting two or more numbers to find the difference. Regrouping is using **one ten** to form **ten ones**, **one hundred** to form **ten tens** and so on.

Look at the examples. Follow the steps to subtract.

Example: 37
              -19

Step 1: Regroup.   **Step 2:** Subtract the ones.   **Step 3:** Subtract the tens.

 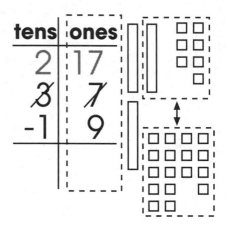 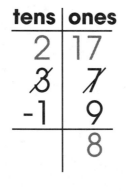 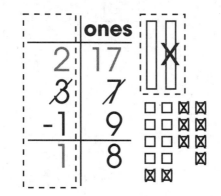 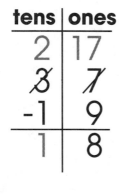 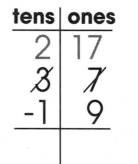

tens	ones
2	17
3̶	7̶
-1	9

tens	ones
2	17
3̶	7̶
-1	9
	8

tens	ones
2	17
3̶	7̶
-1	9
1	8

12	30	52	47	21	45
- 8	-12	-25	-35	-13	-25

Two-Digit Subtraction

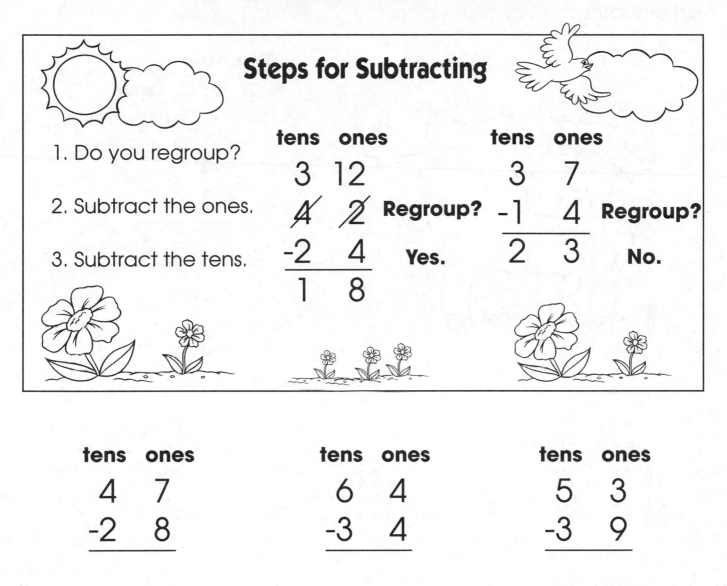

Steps for Subtracting

1. Do you regroup?

2. Subtract the ones.

3. Subtract the tens.

tens	ones
3	12
4̶	2̶
-2	4
1	8

Regroup?

Yes.

tens	ones
3	7
-1	4
2	3

Regroup?

No.

tens	ones
4	7
-2	8

tens	ones
6	4
-3	4

tens	ones
5	3
-3	9

56	83	43	75
-27	-47	-39	-53

73	35	67	26
-66	-14	-58	- 7

Two-Digit Addition and Subtraction

Add or subtract using regrouping.

Example:

	tens	ones
	2	15
	3̸	5
-	2	7
		8

56	40	35	42	97	44	93
-27	-16	+27	-14	-48	+28	-39

56	68	73	33	49	77	27
-17	-49	-24	+18	+32	-68	+19

Two-Digit Addition and Subtraction

Add or subtract using regrouping.

```
  84        41
 -56       -17
```

$$72 + 19 = 91$$

```
  52        84
 -28       -27
```

```
  57        33        64        36
 -39       -15       +17       -19
```

```
  65        48        33        25
 -28       -30       +18       +35
```

Three-Digit Addition

Study the examples. Follow the steps to add.

Examples:

Step 1: Add the ones. **Step 2:** Add the tens. **Step 3:** Add the hundreds.

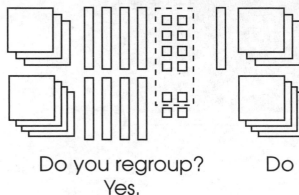 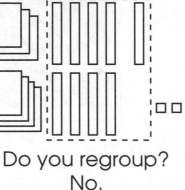 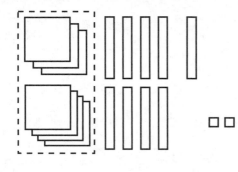

Do you regroup? Do you regroup?
Yes. No.

hundreds	tens	ones	hundreds	tens	ones	hundreds	tens	ones
	1			1			1	
3	4	8	3	4	8	3	4	8
+ 4	4	4	+ 4	4	4	+ 4	4	4
		2		9	2	7	9	2

418   471   334   659   736   426
+323   +319   +528   +127   +145   +165

Three-Digit Addition

Look at the example. Follow the steps to add. Regroup when needed.

Step 1: Add the ones.

Step 2: Add the tens.

Step 3: Add the hundreds.

Example:

hundreds	tens	ones
1	1	
3	4	8
+4	5	4
8	0	2

10 = 1 ten + 1 ones

$$\begin{array}{r} 348 \\ +214 \\ \hline \end{array} \qquad \begin{array}{r} 172 \\ +418 \\ \hline \end{array} \qquad \begin{array}{r} 623 \\ +268 \\ \hline \end{array} \qquad \begin{array}{r} 369 \\ +533 \\ \hline \end{array} \qquad \begin{array}{r} 733 \\ +229 \\ \hline \end{array}$$

$$\begin{array}{r} 411 \\ +299 \\ \hline \end{array} \qquad \begin{array}{r} 423 \\ +169 \\ \hline \end{array} \qquad \begin{array}{r} 624 \\ +368 \\ \hline \end{array} \qquad \begin{array}{r} 272 \\ +469 \\ \hline \end{array} \qquad \begin{array}{r} 393 \\ +418 \\ \hline \end{array}$$

Three-Digit Subtraction

Study the example. Follow the steps to subtract.

Step 1: Regroup the ones if needed.

Step 2: Subtract the ones.

Step 3: Subtract the tens.

Step 4: Subtract the hundreds.

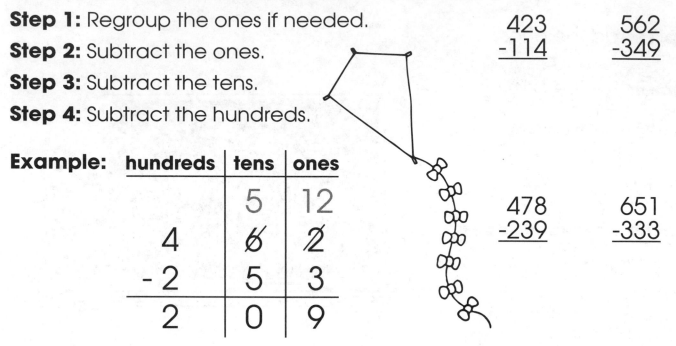

| | 423
-114 | 562
-349 |

Example:

hundreds	tens	ones
	5	12
4	6̶	2̶
- 2	5	3
2	0	9

| | 478
-239 | 651
-333 |

Draw a line to the correct answer. **Color** the kites.

347	144	963	762	287	427
-218	-135	-748	-553	-179	-398

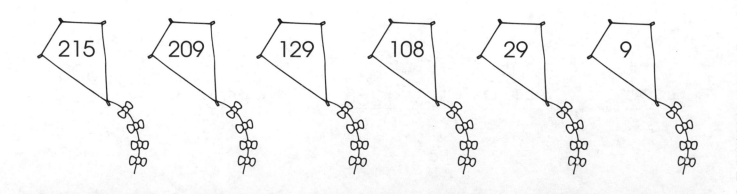

215   209   129   108   29   9

Three-Digit Subtraction

Subtract. Circle the **7's** that appear in the **tens place**.

Example:

$$\begin{array}{r} 492 \\ -221 \\ \hline 2\,⑦\,1 \end{array}$$

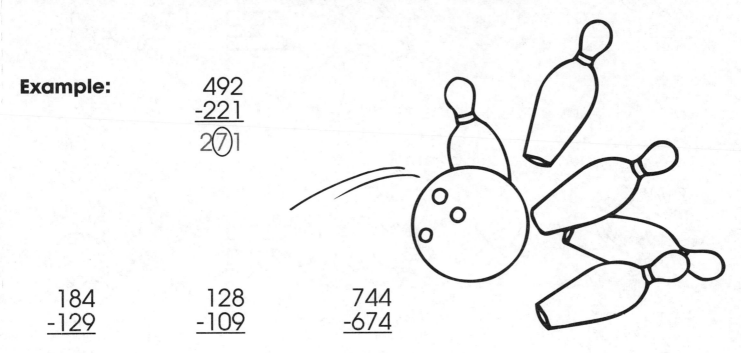

$$\begin{array}{r} 184 \\ -129 \\ \hline \end{array} \qquad \begin{array}{r} 128 \\ -109 \\ \hline \end{array} \qquad \begin{array}{r} 744 \\ -674 \\ \hline \end{array}$$

$$\begin{array}{r} 358 \\ -238 \\ \hline \end{array} \quad \begin{array}{r} 765 \\ -326 \\ \hline \end{array} \quad \begin{array}{r} 584 \\ -435 \\ \hline \end{array} \quad \begin{array}{r} 693 \\ -314 \\ \hline \end{array} \quad \begin{array}{r} 921 \\ -362 \\ \hline \end{array}$$

$$\begin{array}{r} 835 \\ -217 \\ \hline \end{array} \qquad \begin{array}{r} 248 \\ -199 \\ \hline \end{array} \qquad \begin{array}{r} 635 \\ -428 \\ \hline \end{array}$$

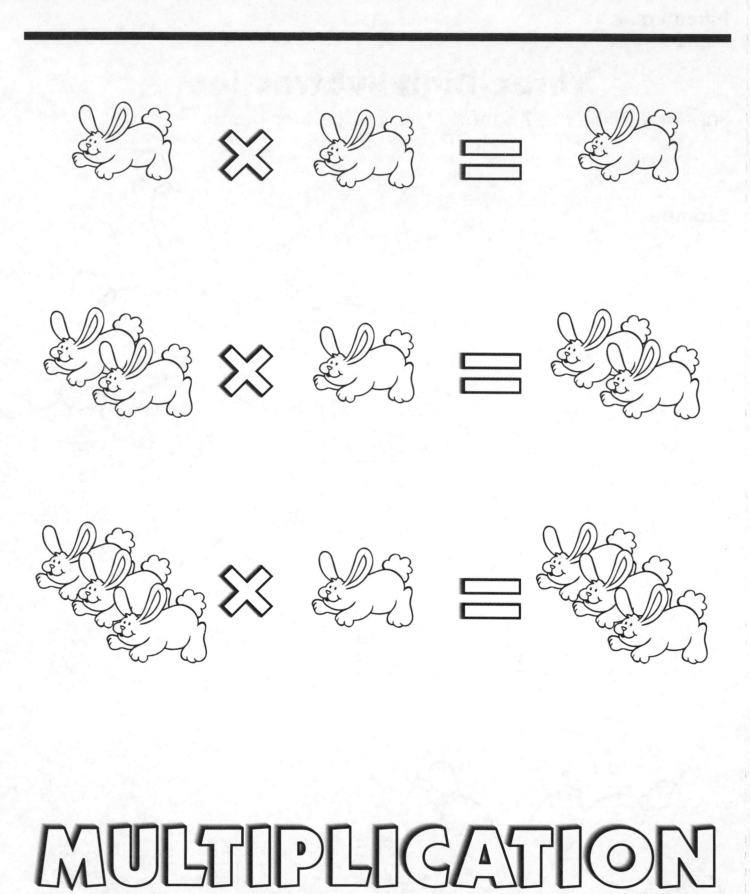

MULTIPLICATION

Multiplication

Multiplication is a short way to find the sum of adding the same number a certain number of times. For example, we write **7 x 4 = 28** instead of **7 + 7 + 7 + 7 = 28**.

Look at the example. Solve the problems.

Example:

3 + 3 + 3 = 9
3 threes = 9
3 x 3 = 9

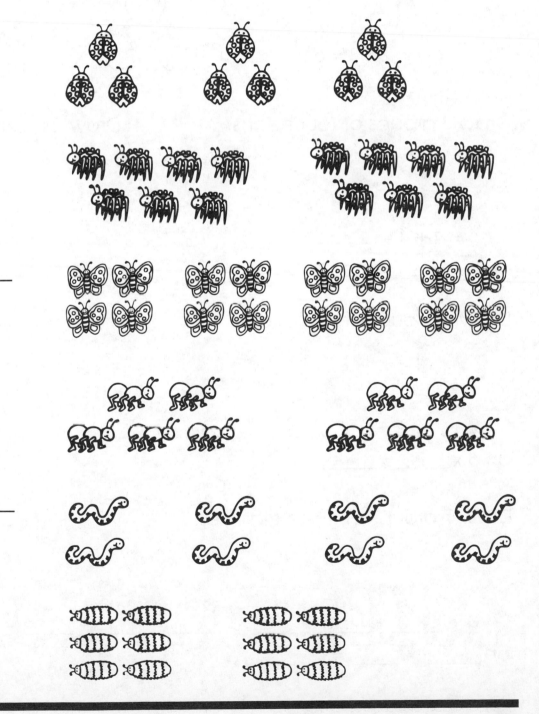

7 + 7 = _____
2 sevens = _____
7 x 2 = _____

4 + 4 + 4 + 4 = _____
4 fours = _____
4 x ___ = _____

5 + 5 = _____
2 fives = _____
2 x ___ = _____

2 + 2 + 2 + 2 = _____
4 twos = _____
4 x ___ = _____

6 + 6 = _____
2 sixes = _____
2 x ___ = _____

Multiplication

Draw a picture for each problem. Then, **write** the missing numbers.

Example:

Draw 2 groups of three apples.

$$3 + 3 = 6$$
$$\text{or } 2 \times 3 = 6$$

Draw 3 groups of four hearts.

Draw 2 groups of five boxes.

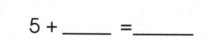

$$4 + 4 + 4 = \underline{\hspace{1cm}}$$
$$\text{or } 3 \times \underline{\hspace{1cm}} = \underline{\hspace{1cm}}$$

$$5 + \underline{\hspace{1cm}} = \underline{\hspace{1cm}}$$
$$\text{or } 2 \times \underline{\hspace{1cm}} = \underline{\hspace{1cm}}$$

Draw 6 groups of two circles.

$$2 + \underline{\hspace{1cm}} + \underline{\hspace{1cm}} + \underline{\hspace{1cm}} + \underline{\hspace{1cm}} + \underline{\hspace{1cm}} = \underline{\hspace{1cm}}$$
$$\text{or } 6 \times \underline{\hspace{1cm}} = \underline{\hspace{1cm}}$$

Draw 7 groups of three triangles.

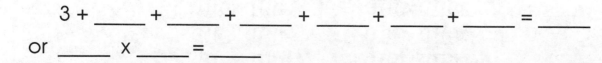

$$3 + \underline{\hspace{1cm}} + \underline{\hspace{1cm}} + \underline{\hspace{1cm}} + \underline{\hspace{1cm}} + \underline{\hspace{1cm}} + \underline{\hspace{1cm}} = \underline{\hspace{1cm}}$$
$$\text{or } \underline{\hspace{1cm}} \times \underline{\hspace{1cm}} = \underline{\hspace{1cm}}$$

Multiplication

Solve the problems.

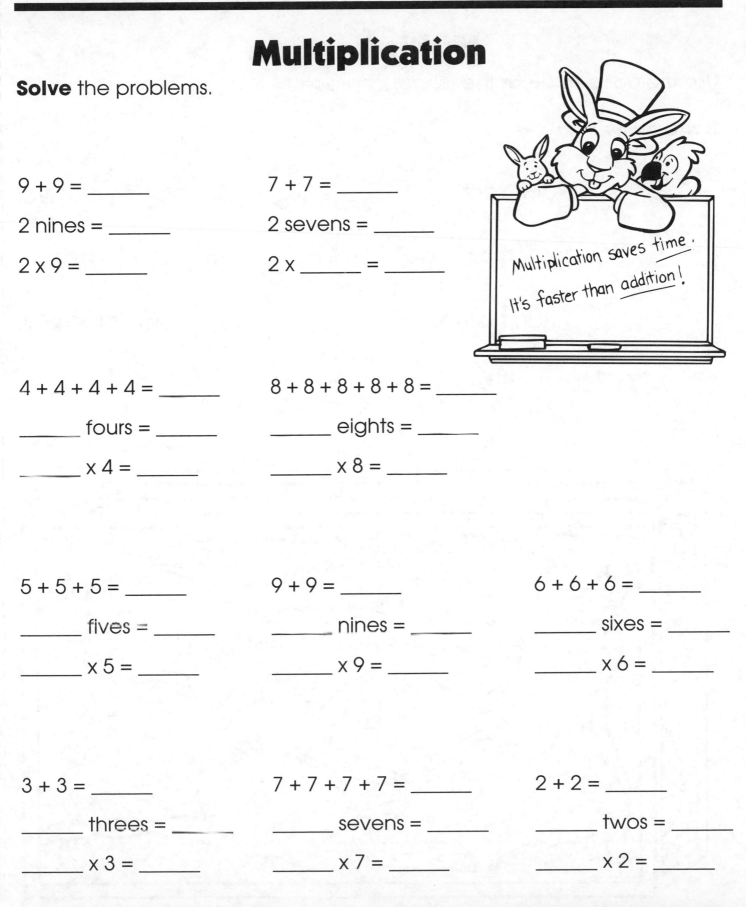

Multiplication saves time.
It's faster than addition!

9 + 9 = _____

2 nines = _____

2 x 9 = _____

7 + 7 = _____

2 sevens = _____

2 x _____ = _____

4 + 4 + 4 + 4 = _____

_____ fours = _____

_____ x 4 = _____

8 + 8 + 8 + 8 + 8 = _____

_____ eights = _____

_____ x 8 = _____

5 + 5 + 5 = _____

_____ fives = _____

_____ x 5 = _____

9 + 9 = _____

_____ nines = _____

_____ x 9 = _____

6 + 6 + 6 = _____

_____ sixes = _____

_____ x 6 = _____

3 + 3 = _____

_____ threes = _____

_____ x 3 = _____

7 + 7 + 7 + 7 = _____

_____ sevens = _____

_____ x 7 = _____

2 + 2 = _____

_____ twos = _____

_____ x 2 = _____

Multiplication

Use the code to **color** the fish.

If the answer is:

 6, color it **red**.

 8, color it **yellow**.

 12, color it **orange**.

 15, color it **green**.

16, color it **blue**.

18, color it **purple**.

27, color it **brown**.

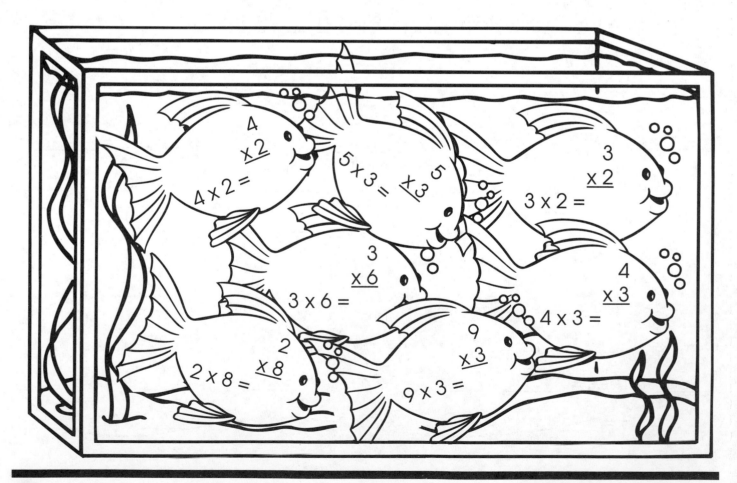

Multiplication

Use the code to **color** the rainbow.

If the answer is:

6, color it **green**.   16, color it **pink**.   25, color it **orange**.

8, color it **purple**.   18, color it **white**.   27, color it **blue**.

9, color it **red**.   21, color it **brown**.

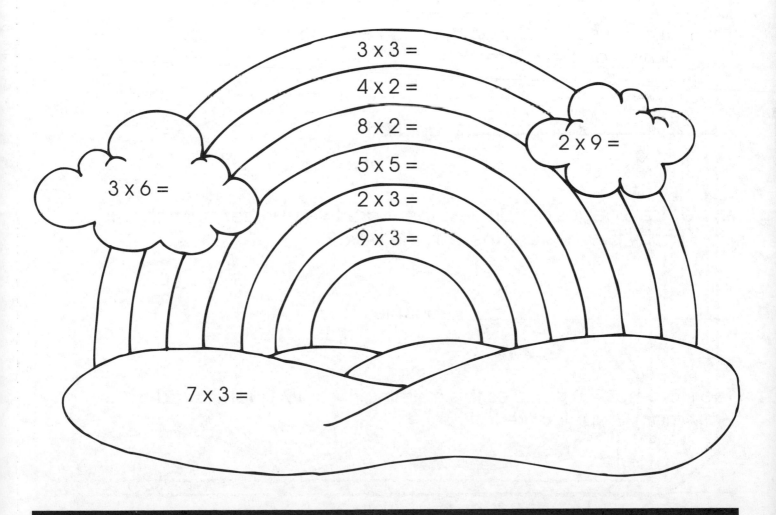

Problem Solving

Tell if you add, subtract or multiply. Then, write the answers. **Hints: In all** means to add. **Left** means to subtract. **Groups with the same number in each** means to multiply.

Example:

There are 6 red birds and 7 blue birds.
How many birds in all?

_____add_____   ____13____ birds

The pet store had 25 goldfish, but 10 were sold.
How many goldfish are left?

_____   _____ goldfish

There are 5 cages of bunnies. There are two bunnies in each cage.
How many bunnies are there in the store?

_____   _____ bunnies

The store had 18 puppies this morning. It sold 7 puppies today.
How many puppies are left?

_____   _____ puppies

Problem Solving

Tell if you add, subtract or multiply. Then,
write the answers.

There were 12 frogs sitting
on a log by a pond, but
3 frogs hopped away.
How many frogs were left?

_____ _____ frogs

There are 9 flowers growing by the pond.
Each flower has 2 leaves.
How many leaves are there?

_____ _____ leaves

A tree had 7 squirrels playing in it. Then, 8 more came along.
How many squirrels are there in all?

_____ _____ squirrels

There were 27 birds living in the trees around the pond, but 9 flew away.
How many birds are left?

_____ _____ birds

GEOMETRY

Circle

A **circle** is a figure that is round. This is a circle: ◯
Find the circles and **draw** a square around them.

Trace the word. Then, **write** the word.

ᴄírᴄle

Square

A **square** is a figure with four corners and four sides of the same length. This is a square:

Find the squares and **draw** a circle around them.

Trace the word. Then, **write** the word.

square

Rectangle

A **rectangle** is a figure with four corners and four sides. The sides opposite each other are the same length. This is a rectangle: ☐

Find the rectangles and **draw** a circle around them.

Trace the word. Then, **write** the word.

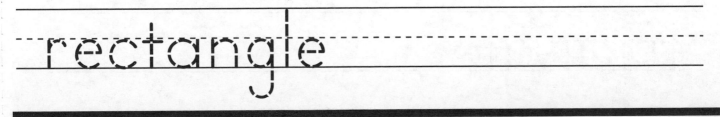

rectangle

Triangle

A **triangle** is a figure with three corners and three sides.
This is a triangle: △

Find the triangles and **draw** a circle around them.

Trace the word. Then, **write** the word.

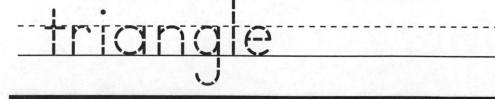

Oval and Diamond

An **oval** is an egg-shaped figure. This is an oval: ◯

A **diamond** is a figure with four sides of the same length. Its corners form points at the top, sides and bottom. This is a diamond: ◇

Find the ovals. **Color** them **red**.
Find the diamonds. **Color** them **blue**.

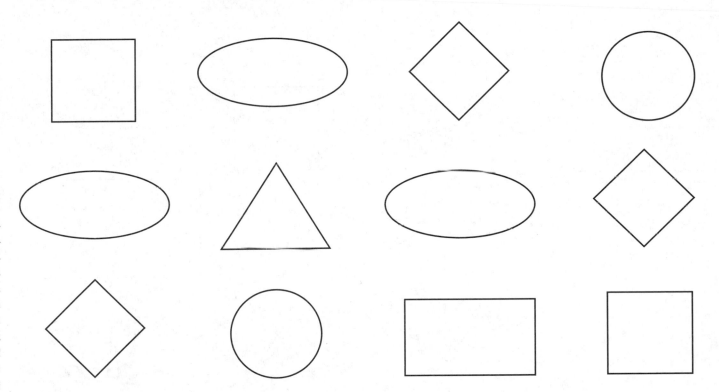

Trace the words. Then, **write** the words.

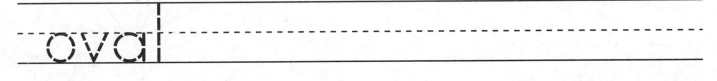

Geometry

Geometry is mathematics that has to do with shapes.

△ Color the **triangles blue**.   ☐ Color the **squares green**.

◯ Color the **circles red**.   ▭ Color the **rectangles pink**.

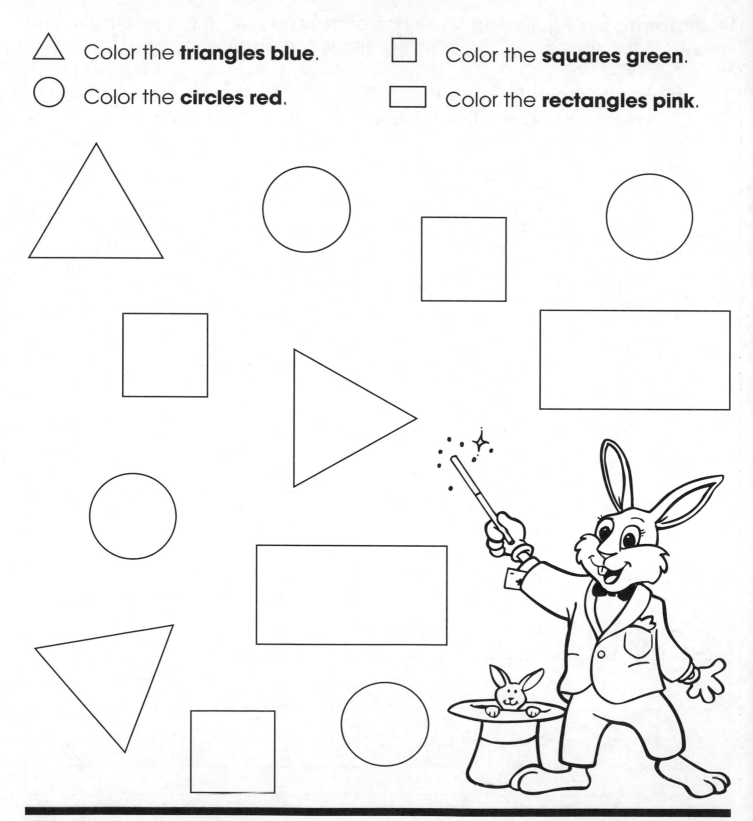

Geometry

Look at your house. Then, draw a picture of the shapes that make up your house. Name the shapes you see.

$\dfrac{3}{4}$ $\dfrac{1}{4}$

$\dfrac{1}{2}$ $\dfrac{2}{4}$ $\dfrac{3}{6}$ $\dfrac{4}{8}$

FRACTIONS

Whole and Half

A **fraction** is a number that names part of a whole, such as $\frac{1}{2}$.

Color half of each object.

Example:

whole apple   half of an apple

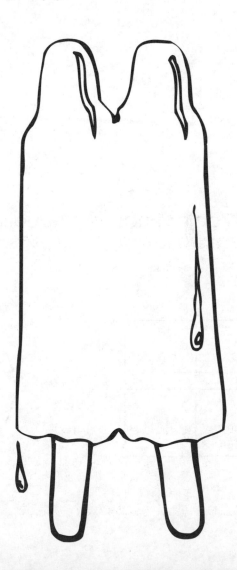

Thirds and Fourths

Each object has three equal parts. **Color one** section.

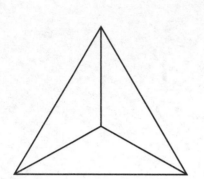  

$$\frac{1}{3}$$

Each object has four equal parts. **Color one** section.

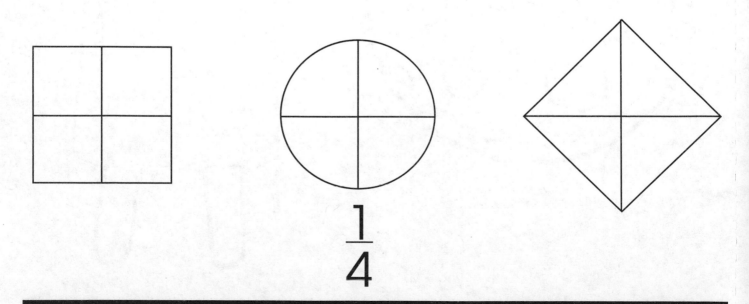

$$\frac{1}{4}$$

Half, Third and Fourth

Count the equal parts. Then, **write** the fraction.

Example:

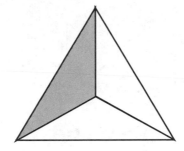

Shaded part = ___1___   Write ___1___
                              ___3___

Equal parts = ___3___

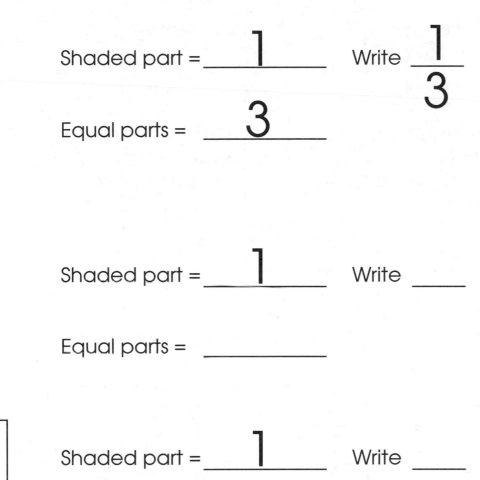

Shaded part = ___1___   Write _____

Equal parts = _____

Shaded part = ___1___   Write _____

Equal parts = _____

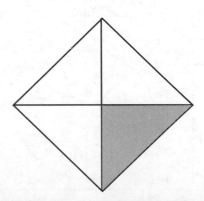

Shaded part = ___1___   Write _____

Equal parts = _____

Half, Third and Fourth

Study the examples. **Color** the correct fraction of each shape.

Examples:

shaded part   1
equal parts   2
$\frac{1}{2}$ **(one-half)**

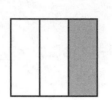

shaded part   1
equal parts   3
$\frac{1}{3}$ **(one-third)**

shaded part   1
equal parts   4
$\frac{1}{4}$ **(one-fourth)**

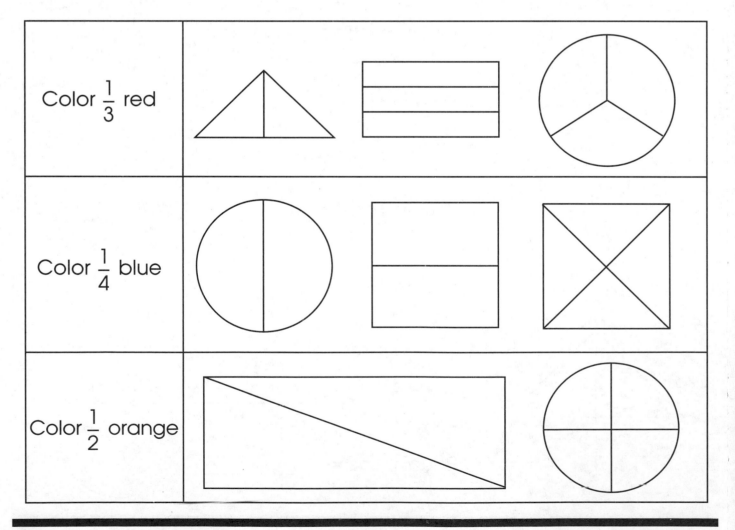

Color $\frac{1}{3}$ red

Color $\frac{1}{4}$ blue

Color $\frac{1}{2}$ orange

Fractions

Draw a line from the fraction to the correct shape.

$\frac{1}{4}$ shaded

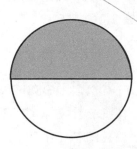

$\frac{2}{4}$ shaded

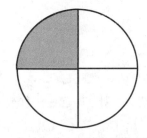

$\frac{1}{2}$ shaded

$\frac{1}{3}$ shaded

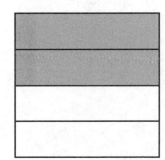

$\frac{2}{3}$ shaded

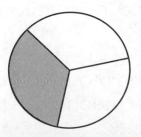

Problem Solving

Read each problem. Use the pictures to help you solve the problem.
Write the fraction that answers the question.

Simon and Jessie shared a pizza.
Together they ate $\frac{3}{4}$ of the pizza.
How much of the pizza is left? _____

Sylvia baked a cherry pie. She gave $\frac{1}{3}$
to her grandmother and $\frac{1}{3}$ to a
friend. How much of the pie did she keep? _____

Timmy erased $\frac{1}{2}$ of the blackboard
before the bell rang for recess. How
much of the blackboard does he have
left to erase? _____

Read the problem. Draw your own picture to help you solve the problem.
Write the fraction that answers the question.

Sarah mowed $\frac{1}{4}$ of the yard before lunch.
How much does she have left to mow? _____

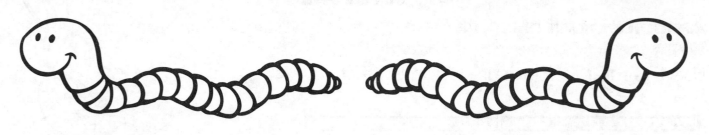

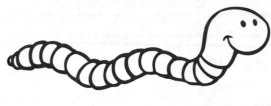

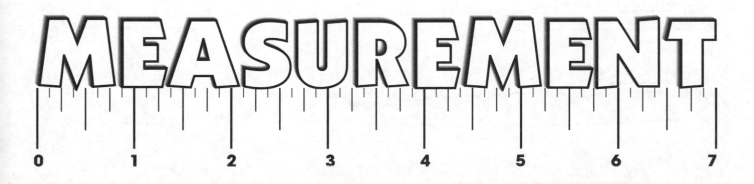

MEASUREMENT

0 1 2 3 4 5 6 7

Inches

An **inch** is a unit of length.

Use this ruler to measure each object.

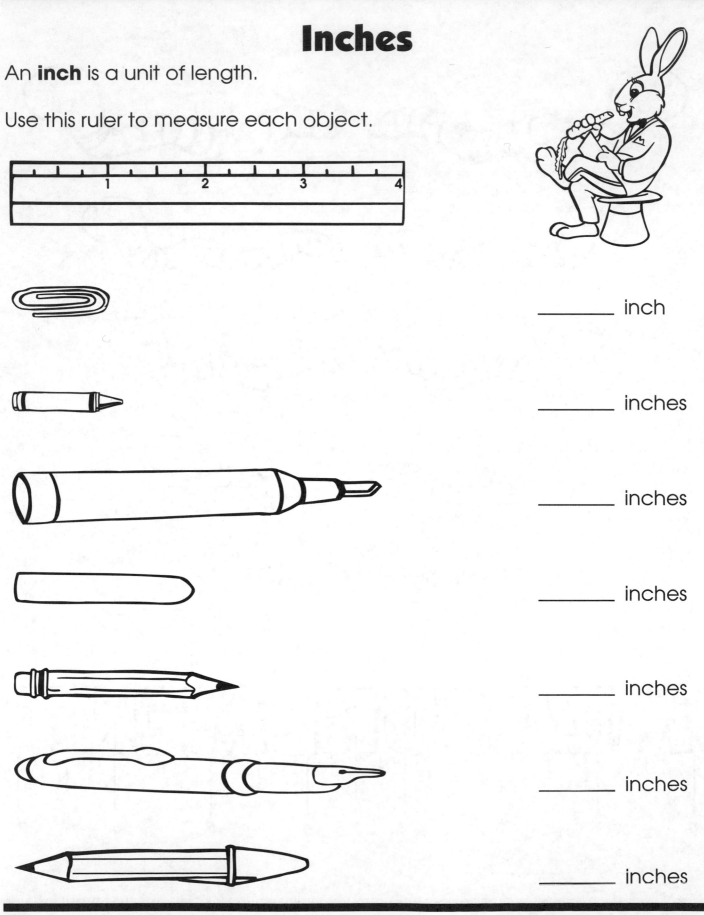

_____ inch

_____ inches

_____ inches

_____ inches

_____ inches

_____ inches

_____ inches

Inches

Use an inch ruler to **measure** the fish to the nearest inch.

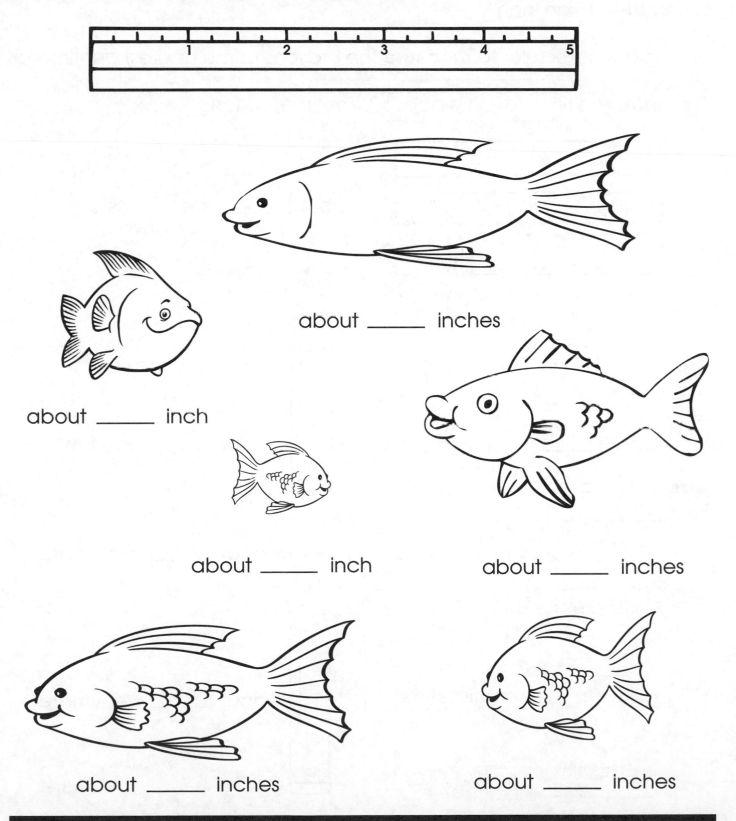

about _____ inches

about _____ inch

about _____ inch

about _____ inches

about _____ inches

about _____ inches

Centimeters

A **centimeter** is a unit of length in the metric system. There are 2.54 centimeters in an inch.

Use a centimeter ruler to **measure** the crayons to the nearest centimeter.

Example: The first crayon is about 7 centimeters long.

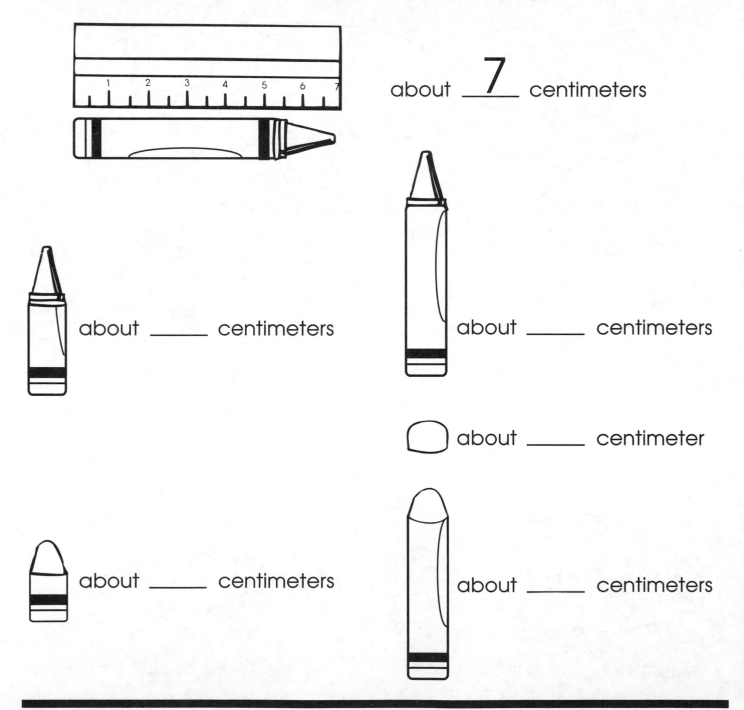

about ___7___ centimeters

about _____ centimeters

about _____ centimeters

about _____ centimeter

about _____ centimeters

about _____ centimeters

Centimeters

The giraffe is about 8 centimeters high. How many centimeters (cm) high are the paintbrushes? **Write** your answer in the blanks.

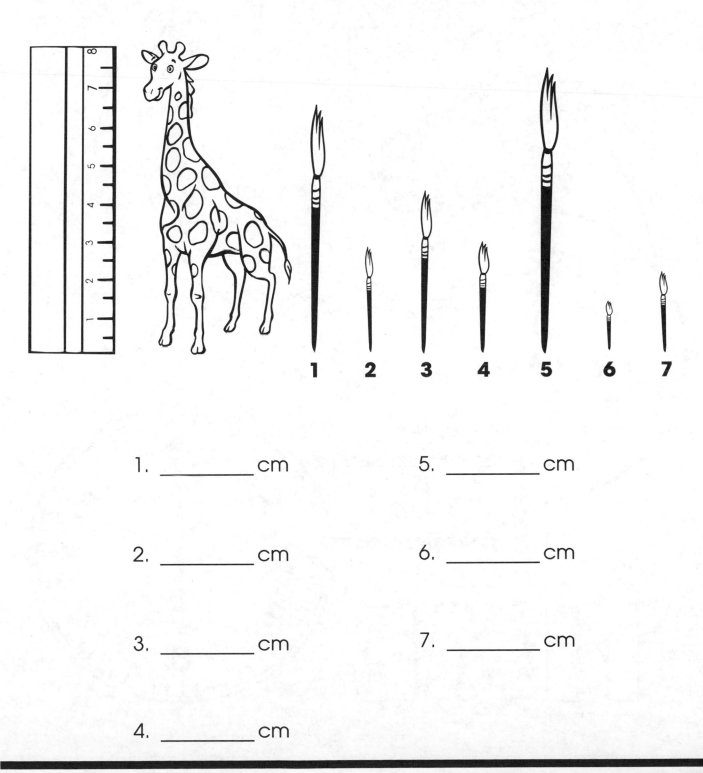

1. _____ cm   5. _____ cm

2. _____ cm   6. _____ cm

3. _____ cm   7. _____ cm

4. _____ cm

TIME

Parts of a Clock

A clock can tell you what time it is. A clock has different parts. Read and trace each part of the clock.

numbers

face

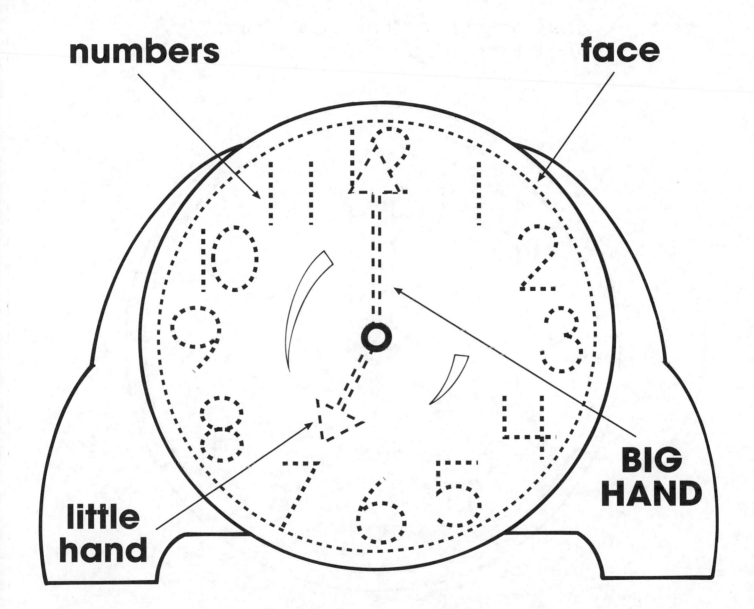

BIG HAND

little hand

The **BIG HAND** is on 12.

The **little hand** tells the hour.

Time to the Hour

An **hour** is **sixty minutes** long. It takes an hour for the big hand to go around the clock. When the big hand is on 12, and the little hand points to a number, that is the hour!

The big hand is on the 12. Color it **red**.
The little hand is on the 8. Color it **blue**.

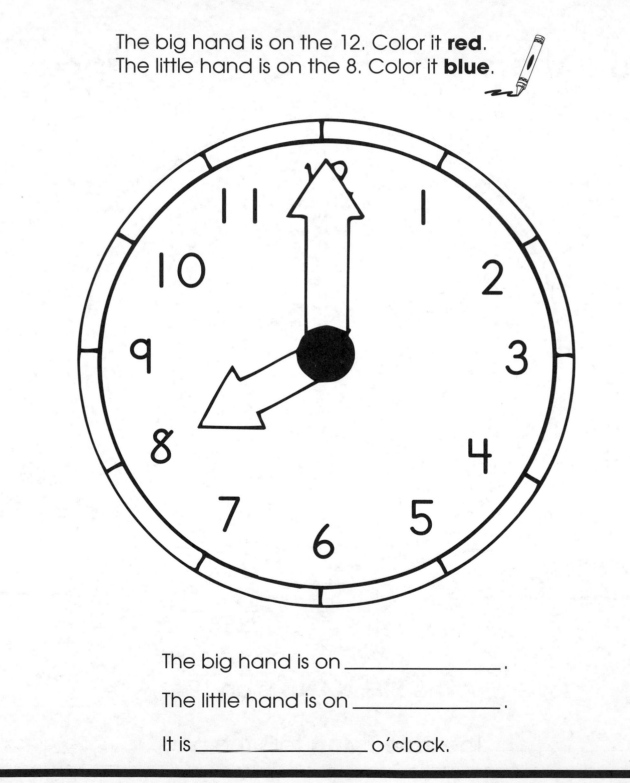

The big hand is on _____.

The little hand is on _____.

It is _____ o'clock.

Time to the Hour

Color the little hour hand **red**. Fill in the blanks.

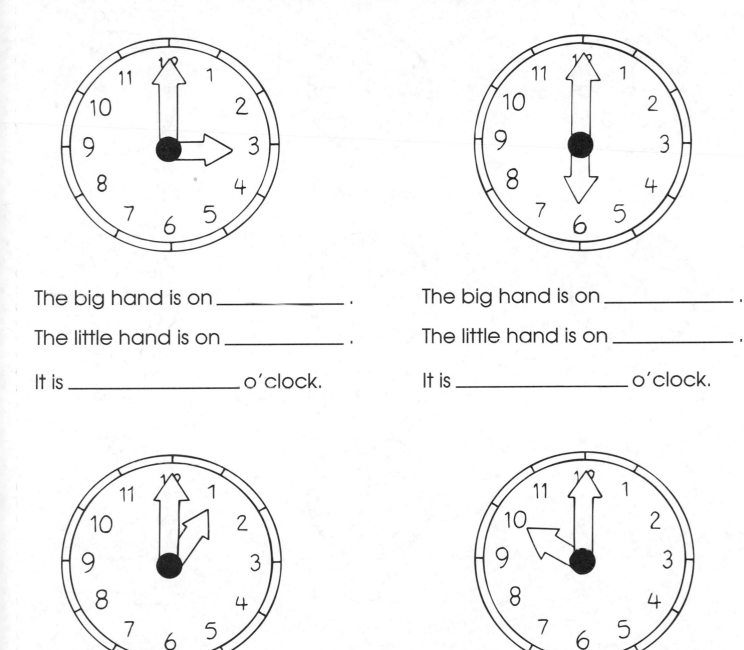

The big hand is on _____ .

The little hand is on _____ .

It is _____ o'clock.

The big hand is on _____ .

The little hand is on _____ .

It is _____ o'clock.

The big hand is on _____ .

The little hand is on _____ .

It is _____ o'clock.

The big hand is on _____ .

The little hand is on _____ .

It is _____ o'clock.

Time to the Hour

What is the time?

_____o'clock

_____o'clock

_____o'clock

_____o'clock

_____o'clock

_____o'clock

_____o'clock

_____o'clock

_____o'clock

_____o'clock

_____o'clock

_____o'clock

Digital Clocks

This is a digital clock. It shows the hour, then the minutes.

Draw the little hour hand on the face clock below to read 10 o'clock.

Both clocks show that it is 10 o'clock. Make a **green circle** around the clocks you have at home.

Digital Clocks

Write the time on the digital clocks.

Time

Show each time two ways. **Draw** the hands on each clock face. **Write** the time on each digital clock.

A.   Bessie Bear gets up at 6 o'clock.

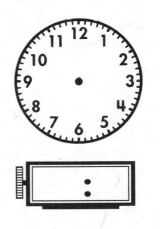

B.   Bernie Bear eats breakfast at 7 o'clock.

C.   What time do you get up on school mornings?
     Draw it here!

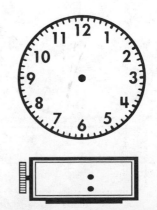

Time to the Half-Hour

This clock face shows the time gone by since 8'clock.

Thirty minutes or half an hour have gone by.

There are three ways to say time to the half-hour.
We say seven-thirty, thirty past seven or half past seven.

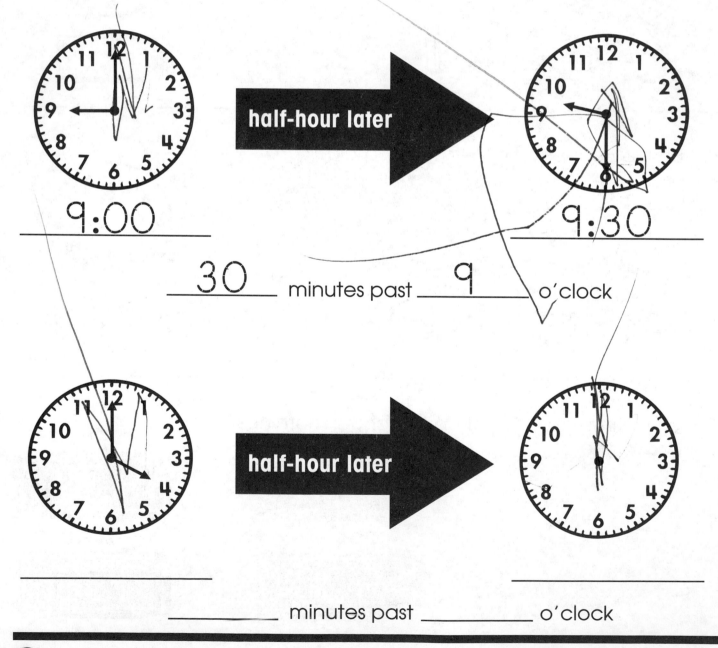

9:00   → half-hour later →   9:30

_30_ minutes past _9_ o'clock

half-hour later

_____ minutes past _____ o'clock

Time to the Half-Hour

half-hour later

_____   _____

_____ minutes past _____ o'clock

half-hour later

_____   _____

_____ minutes past _____ o'clock

What is your dinner time?
Circle the time you eat.

4:30	6:30
5:30	7:30

Practice

What time is it?

Time to the Quarter-Hour

Each hour is 60 minutes long. An hour has 4 quarter-hours. A quarter-hour is 15 minutes long.

This clock face shows a quarter of an hour. From the 12 to the 3 is 15 minutes.

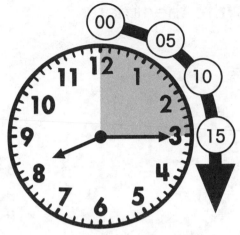

Trace the hands of the clock to show 8:15. **Color** the big minute hand **blue**. **Color** the little hour hand **red**. From the 12 to the 3 is 15 minutes.

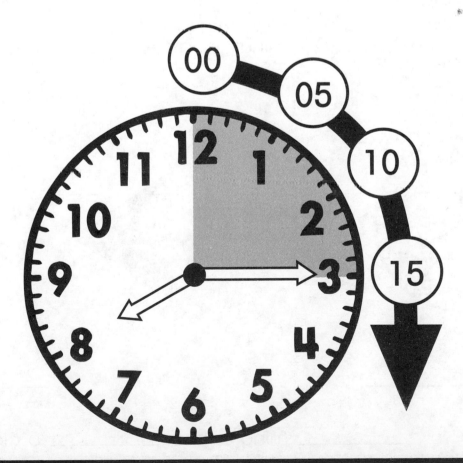

Time to the Quarter-Hour

Each hour has 4 quarter-hours. A quarter-hour is 15 minutes long.

Write the times.

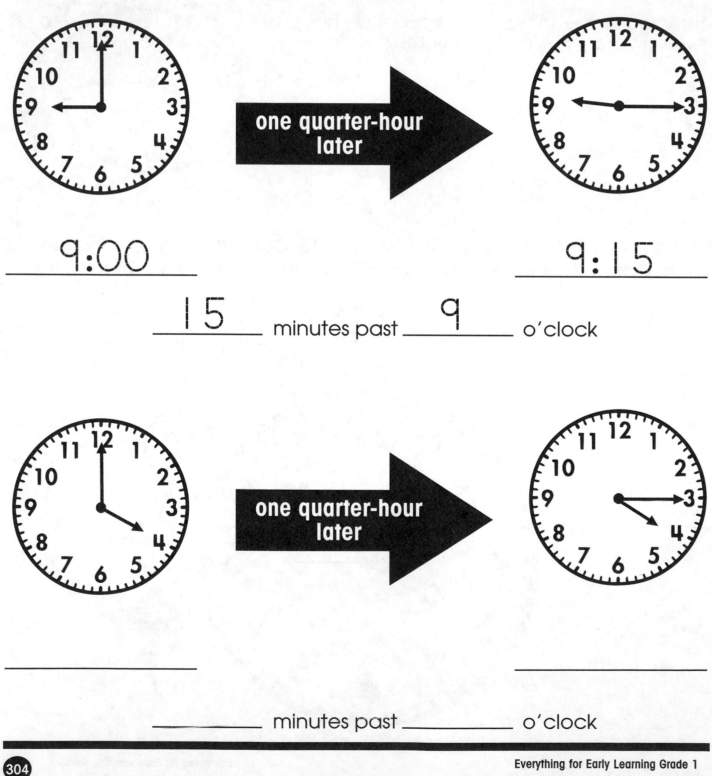

9:00

one quarter-hour later

9:15

__15__ minutes past __9__ o'clock

one quarter-hour later

_____ minutes past _____ o'clock

Time to the Quarter-Hour

Draw the hands. **Write** the times.

5:15

___15___ minutes after

___5___ o'clock

10:15

_____ minutes after

_____ o'clock

2:15

_____ minutes after

_____ o'clock

9:15

_____ minutes after

_____ o'clock

Time to the Quarter-Hour

Your digital clock has quarter-hours, too! It also shows 15 minutes.

Time to the Quarter-Hour

Count the numbers by 5's. **Write** how many minutes have passed.

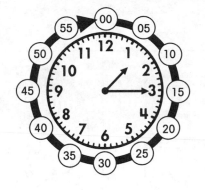

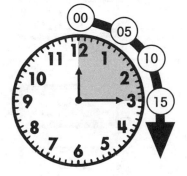

___15___ minutes after ___12___ o'clock

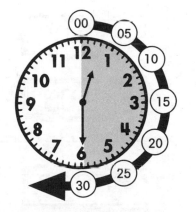

_____ minutes after _____ o'clock

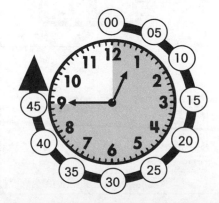

_____ minutes after _____ o'clock

Time to the Quarter-Hour

Circle the correct time.

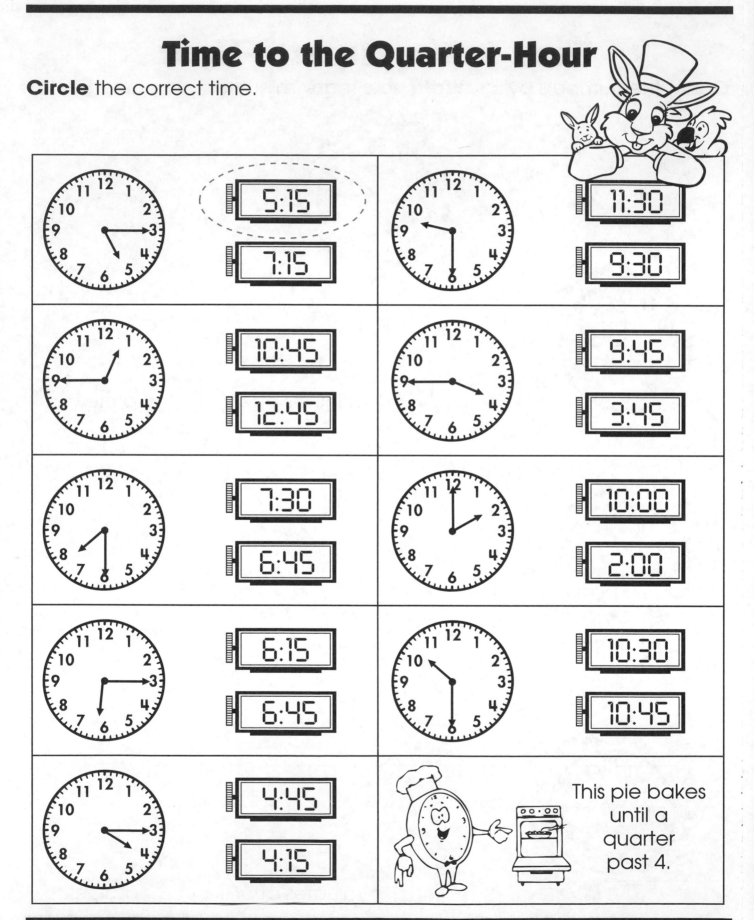

5:15 (circled) / 7:15	11:30 / 9:30
10:45 / 12:45	9:45 / 3:45
7:30 / 6:45	10:00 / 2:00
6:15 / 6:45	10:30 / 10:45
4:45 / 4:15	This pie bakes until a quarter past 4.

Time to the Quarter-Hour

Draw the hands on each clock face. **Write** the times.

A. Alberto begins working in the yard at 10:00. He stops 45 minutes later.

Begins   Stops

_____:_____   _____:_____

_____   _____

B. Darlene begins playing catch at 2:30. She stops 15 minutes later.

Begins   Stops

_____:_____   _____:_____

_____   _____

C. Write your own story.

_____

_____

_____

Begins   Stops

_____:_____   _____:_____

_____   _____

Pennies

One **penny** is worth **one cent**. Each piece of candy costs 1¢. **Cut out** each money box and **glue** it beside the candy it will buy.

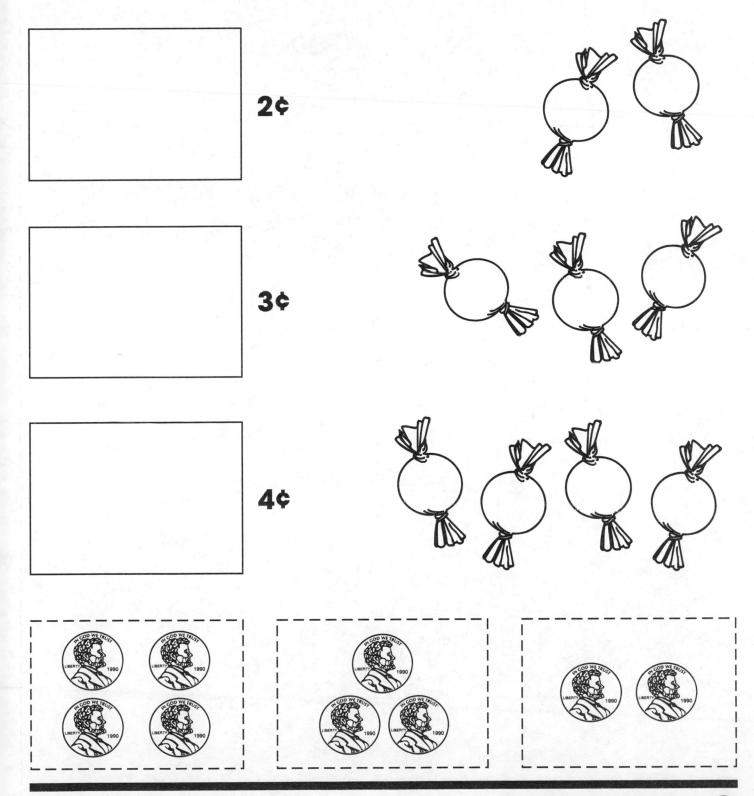

2¢

3¢

4¢

Page is blank for cutting exercise on previous page.

Pennies

Count the pennies. **Write** the amount.

_____ pennies =_____ ¢

_____ pennies =_____ ¢

_____ penny =_____ ¢

Nickels

One **nickel** is worth **five cents**.

Look at the two sides of a nickel.
Color the nickels silver.

_____1_____ nickel = _____5_____ pennies

_____1_____ nickel = _____5_____ cents

_____1_____ nickel = _____5_____ ¢

5¢ = _____¢ + _____¢ + _____¢ + _____¢ + _____¢

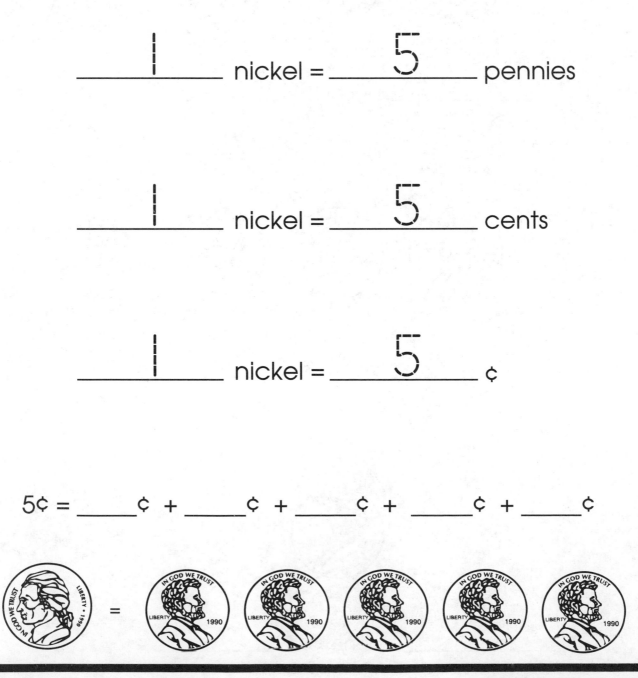

Nickels and Pennies

Count the money. Start with the nickel. Then, count the pennies. **Write** the amount.

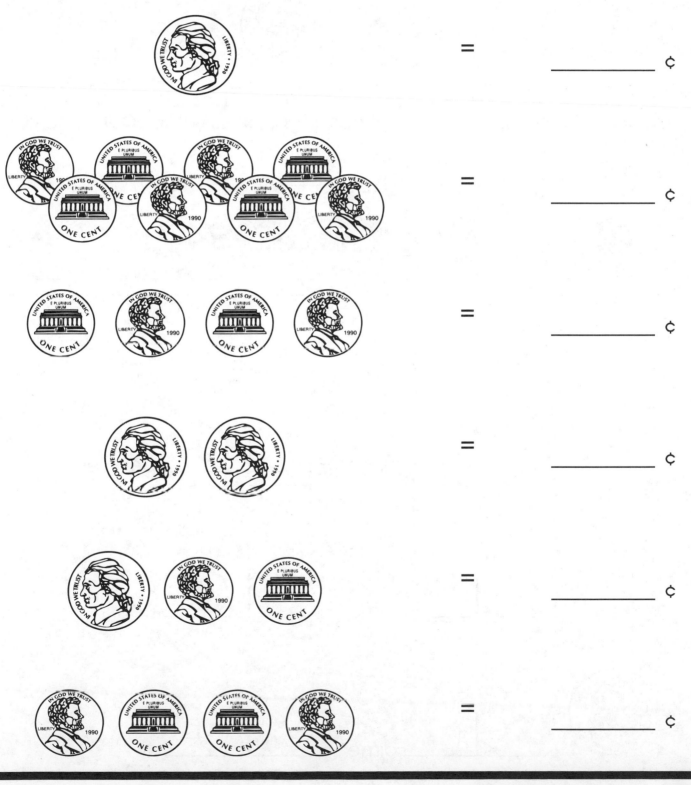

=　　_____ ¢

=　　_____ ¢

=　　_____ ¢

=　　_____ ¢

=　　_____ ¢

=　　_____ ¢

Dime

One **dime** is worth **ten cents**.

Each side of a dime is different. It has ridges on its edge. **Color** the dime **silver**.

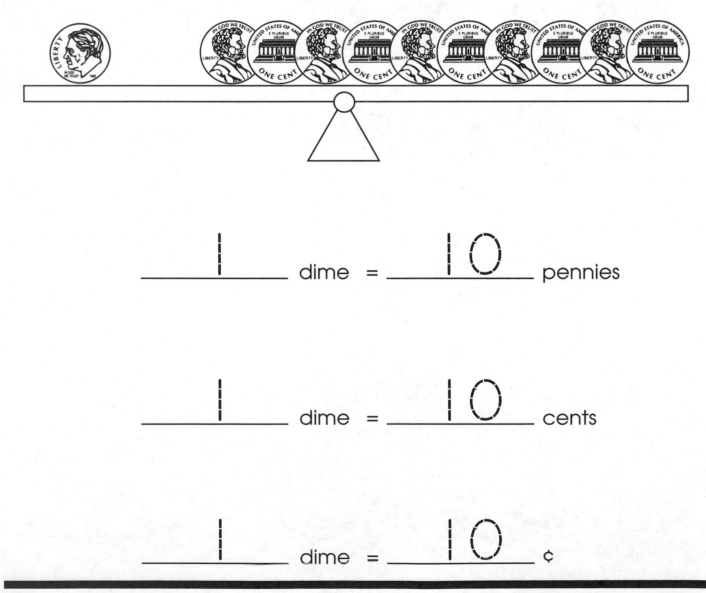

_____1_____ dime = _____10_____ pennies

_____1_____ dime = _____10_____ cents

_____1_____ dime = _____10_____ ¢

Dimes, Nickels and Pennies

Count the money. Start with the dime. Then, count the nickels and pennies.
Write the amount.

A.

_____ ¢

B.

_____ ¢

Quarters

One **quarter** is worth **twenty-five cents**. Our first President, George Washington, is on the front. The eagle is on the back.

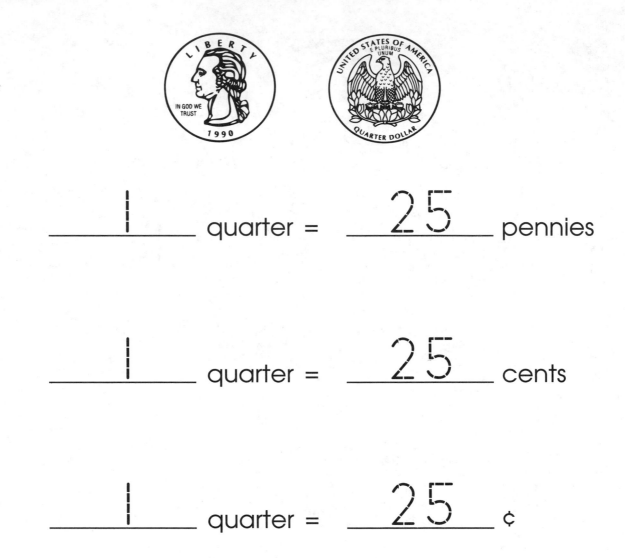

__1__ quarter = __25__ pennies

__1__ quarter = __25__ cents

__1__ quarter = __25__ ¢

Count these nickels by fives. Is this another way to make a quarter?

yes   no

Quarters, Dimes, Nickels and Pennies

Match the money with the amount.

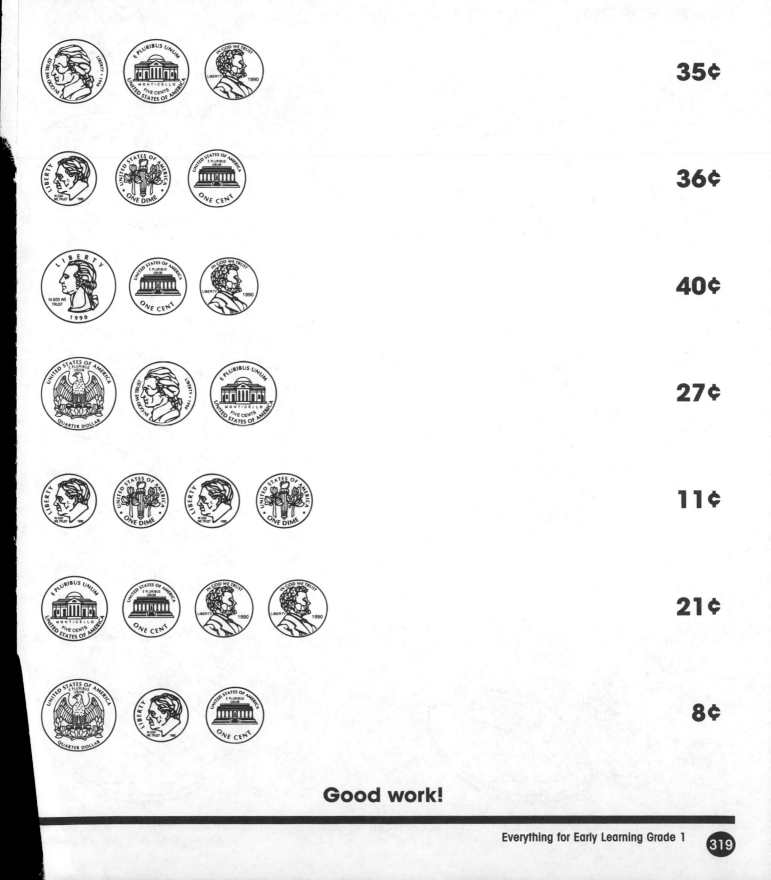

35¢

36¢

40¢

27¢

11¢

21¢

8¢

Good work!

Quarters, Dimes, Nickels and Pennies

Count the coins. Start with the quarters. **Write** the amount in each football.

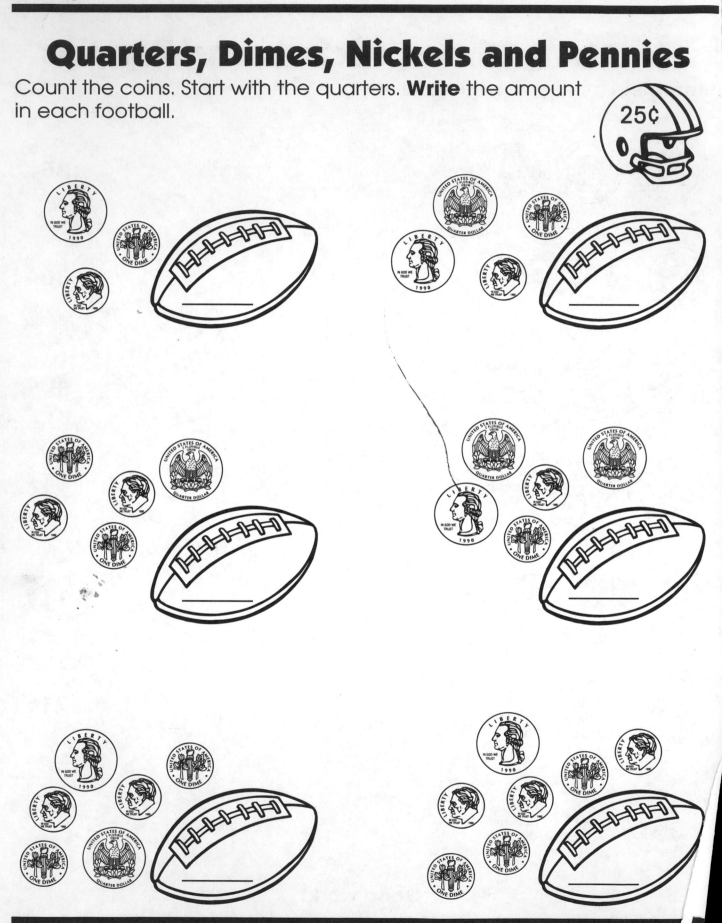